D0842302

WED
4.98

Your
Private
World

A Chronicle Book

Your

Private World

A Study of Intimate Gardens

by Thomas Church

Chronicle Books / San Francisco

A Division of the Chronicle Publishing Company

Copyright 1969 by Thomas D. Church

Library of Congress Card No. 74-99220

*All rights reserved. No part of this book may be reproduced
in any form without written permission from the publishers.*

Photographers: Morley Baer, Ernest Braun, Thomas D. Church,
Philip Fein, Bruce Harlow, Emelie D. Nicholson,
Maynard Parker, Rondal Partridge, Karl H. Riek,
John Robinson, Ezra Stoller, Roger Sturtevant

(A complete listing for each picture appears on pages 201 and 202)

Design by Wolfgang Lederer

Type by Holmes Typography Inc., San Jose, Calif.

Printing by Peninsula Lithograph, Menlo Park, Calif.

Binding by Cardoza Bindery, San Francisco

Contents

Thomas Church

Introduction

We have been in the business of residential landscape design for close to 40 years, and it is safe to say that the profession has gone through several revolutions in that space of time.

Western living created one kind of revolution, and the garden became as much a year-round living environment as the house. And then there came a time, in the 1940s, when it was easier to get a janitor than a gardener, and our gardens had to change again.

The demand was for more low-maintenance materials, even asphalt, and our job was to find ways of making it beautiful. And then came post-war technology, and suddenly we had a whole range of new materials and techniques to stimulate our thinking and broaden our horizons.

*Introduction
(continued)*

PART 1 *Gardens*

And people have certainly changed. Today's young home-buyer looks for advantages and features his father didn't even care about—and because we are not designing to fit academic abstracts but to suit people, our designs must change as needs change.

And, especially lately, we are asked about the trends. It was never an easy question to answer, and now it has become impossible. The only trend we can see is a trend away from trends. People are worrying less about fashion in homes and landscapes and more about what pleases them and serves the needs of their family best.

I could say that all our clients insist on well-defined entrance courts with plenty of parking near an inviting front door. But there are clients who live informally, yearn for rustic gardens and want the automobile as far away as possible. They feel that guests like a little hike before dinner and they've bought steep hillsides to prove it.

(I personally prefer people who are still breathing when they arrive and relaxed enough to wonder about the wine. I don't want them to see it cooling before dinner because they've mistaken the kitchen door for the entrance.)

Of course, good building sites that allow for all the amenities are no longer easy to find. Sometimes we think of new

PART 3 *Landscaping the Entrance*

PART 2 *Remodeling the Old Garden*

PART 4 *Fences, Screens and Stairs*

ways to provide them on property whose drama demands it. A while back, we designed a garden on a beach in Southern California at the foot of a high cliff. Parking is at the top and a hillevator does the hiking.

I considered mentioning that everyone likes to entertain on a solid terrace just outside the living room. But I remembered a flagstone terrace, recently installed, with herbs and alpines blooming between the stones. It's hard to walk on and impossible to furnish, but it is beautiful. Reducing glare, it brings controlled softness and color up to the living room glass. The main terrace is out in the garden under the shade of an oak. The family seems to enjoy it.

3

Introduction
(continued)

PART 5 *Trees*

PART 7 *Decks and Yards*

PART 8 *Work and Storage Areas*

Again, I thought of writing that gardens seem to be more formally organized than they were 25 years ago when we were all experimenting with free forms and abstractions. I could even have supported it with many current examples that recall European gardens and reflect my appreciation of their strength and sensitivities. But we recently completed one of the most casual gardens I've ever done. There's not a center-line axis in sight. But it will be restful and will look, I hope, as though it had happened one day when no one was looking.

It is also said that everyone now wants a swimming pool. We've contributed to that myth by designing several hundred

4

PART 6 *Swimming Pools*

PART 9 *Children's Play Areas*

during the past 25 years. Some have simple settings with open-air dressing rooms and others are complexes rivaling a country club. But we also continue to do many gardens for clients who want peace and quiet. Other families have figured out that the community pool or established club nearby is more carefree. Some people prefer to spend their money on milk or bourbon; for while chlorine is not a glamorous liquid, pools consume it by the gallon.

I would suggest that the trend toward low maintenance has now become a necessity. I can't be sure of any new design approach that agrees on how to achieve it. I once thought that a large expanse of paving was the obvious solution, but now clients are complaining more and more frequently that janitorial help (including teenage sons and daughters) is as hard to find as gardeners. Sometimes I think grass is the answer, particularly in regions where rains do all the watering. But a while back I completed a summer place where 5000 square feet was planted in petunias. It was a bright splash on the countryside and quite free of maintenance—for almost six months.

And now, various vocational training programs are starting which may give us an entire new generation of gardeners. Perhaps the pendulum is swinging back the other way, and in 20 years gardening will once more be largely back in the

5

hands of the professionals. If so, we might again compare long-term maintenance with initial expenditures for construction and, coming full circle, arrive back at the old rule-of-thumb.

Alas, there is one trend which is almost sure to continue, and to which I can find no significant exceptions: rising costs. They seem to be going up quicker and higher than hemlines. But wages are going up, too (the famous wage-price spiral, I suppose), so the cost rise has very little ultimate effect on gardens and the trend away from trends.

Finally, if this book has any overall message, it is that the trend away from trends is a good one. To reiterate a point I have made elsewhere, gardens *are* for people. In every case, they should please and serve the people who live in them. There is a wide variety of ideas in this book, and all were designed with the people who would be affected by the ideas in mind. There are no dogmas that are unbreakable—the only limit to your garden is at the boundaries of your imagination.

1

Gardens

A garden is, no more, no less, what you make it. It can be an albatross around your neck—expensive to create, time-consuming to maintain, so filled with fragile plants and uncomfortable corners that your guests feel constrained to tiptoe around your yard, whispering for fear the whole unlikely edifice will topple of its own weight.

Or your garden can be as bland as oatmeal, a broad flat expanse of grass bounded by a nice dull fence. Great for football but it gives the guest everything it has to offer—visually and functionally—in seven seconds.

If you have one of these kinds of gardens, chances are you inherited it in some manner, either through inadvertence or indifference, and you've been afraid to do anything about it. Perhaps you think it's hopeless, perhaps you think it's too difficult; perhaps (and this is most likely) you know you don't like what you've got, but you don't know where you should start to change it. And furthermore you suspect there are rules you might break.

The place to start is with yourself. Decide what you like in a garden, and what you need—then look around for ideas. This first chapter is intended to give you an overview of the possibilities inherent in the common, or garden variety, garden. There are a wide range of materials and techniques available; here we will mention a few of the more popular and interesting.

For instance, several of the examples (like "The Illusion of Space," "Be Bold in Design," "Borrow a Landscape" and "Camouflage Attractively") remind us that things are not always what they seem, and that one should not be reluctant to use a little benign deception to a good end. And these same examples along with some others ("Design Provides The Answer to Complex Demands," "A Secluded Rooftop Haven," "Expand Toward the Street" and "The Minimal Garden") show us that a garden can be anywhere.

"Bridge The Gap" completes this chapter with a reminder that it is possible, even desirable, to use the disadvantages of your lot to your own advantage—in other words, to work with the land, its natural character and substance, rather than against it.

Another, often overlooked, feature of gardens is their emotional character. "Be Bold in Design" and "Design It for Sweep" illustrate the advantages of being firm and lofty in approach, designing the garden for sweep and total effect. Small thinkers get small gardens. And "Create a Calm Composition reminds us that gardens can generate an emotion—a cluttered, random, untended garden can arouse feelings of dislike and discomfort, while a garden in harmony with itself and its surroundings can give the viewer an immediate feeling of serenity and peace.

Most of the other examples deal with specific techniques and materials. We consider the use of mathematics ("Make It Geometric") in a successful garden, and we look into the problem of what kind of flowers should be used in the garden, and what designs work well with what plants ("Dedicate Your Garden To Springtime," "It's Work But Worth It" and "Picking Your Plants").

One example delves into the question of vistas from inside the house ("Plant to Use Your Window"), while another considers the house as part of the environment of the garden ("Plant It Away"). One takes on ivy, while another deals with hedges, including the delicate problem of knowing what to separate and what to include.

In all of the examples, the underlying idea is that any problem in any garden yields a solution, given enough time and thought. There are big gardens and little gardens, city gardens and country gardens, appealingly busy gardens and serenely simple gardens—and, alas, there are also ugly gardens. But ugly gardens can be changed, which is what this chapter is all about.

Dedicate Your Garden
to Springtime

Gardens are planned to provide for the various interests and moods of the people who will use and enjoy them. Some will request a garden which looks essentially the same 12 months of the year when they realize that keeping the excitement in a low key is also the answer to minimum maintenance.

Others will want to grow the flower of the month and feel that a garden should be a show of brilliance from January 1 to December 31, inclusive. This taxes all of us—the landscape architect, the nurseryman and the client. Perpetual color in the garden is a full-time pursuit, with results that cannot be guaranteed.

The compromise client is one whom I understand. He is dedicated to springtime and lets the rest of the year take care of itself. This does not mean that the garden need be completely dull for nine months of the year, but it helps in any situation to narrow the field, and his choice is logical in any climate.

Other seasons seem to merge together, but spring is different; there is no problem in recognizing it when it arrives in the garden. And for the devoted, it is a season which lasts six months, since it begins with dreaming over catalogs and the fall planting. The anticipation is only equaled by the more tangible reward of the first crocus when "suddenly, it's spring!"

With this emphasis on the spring season, the garden has a theme which influences the selection of permanent materials used in creating it. For while the color, texture and scale of the paving, walls, steps and background plantings may vary, they should be chosen to complement the palette and fragile quality of the blossoms which are to be featured.

Shown here are south gardens whose walls and steps, of water-worn stone, accent the arch of a crabapple and create a subtly colored setting for the bright azaleas, delicate alpines and spiky bulbs which signify springtime in San Francisco.

*Perpetual color is a fulltime
pursuit, but even amateurs can
dedicate their gardens to springtime.*

Designed for Jean Wolff, San Francisco

Designed for Mrs. Daniel Volkmann, San Francisco

Designed for Mr. & Mrs. Maurice Goldman, San Francisco

*Choose the color and texture of
the walls and steps to complement
the fragile beauty of the blossoms.*

Designed for Mr. & Mrs. Austin Earl, Atherton

It's Work But Worth It

The annual flower border is fast disappearing from our scene. It means planning, work and seasonal gaps when the ground is bare. Yet nothing can equal the exuberance of growth and riot of color through summer and fall that annuals can offer. A border of stocks, snapdragons, larkspur and zinnias, edged by petunias, ageratum, alyssum and lobelia can provide a soul-satisfying summer with a minimum of work.

Average suburbanites today plead that they have neither a green thumb nor the time to cultivate flowers. Give us, they say, some of those wonderful perennials that bloom all year and take no care at all. What books do they read? It took the 19th Century English headgardener (with nine helpers) to create the perennial border that became one of the wonders of the modern world.

Affluent Americans have been able to reproduce it, and dedicated gardeners (hours: nine to five daily) can produce admirable results but—for maximum color per dollar and man-hour—buy a few flats of annuals. If you're willing to accept bulbs and flowering shrubs in the spring and bare ground in the winter, the summer annuals (a long and exciting list) can provide vibrant color through the rest of the year.

Though on the wane,
a border of hardy annuals
can add a profusion of color
to the perimeter of a walk,
or against the base
of a dividing fence.

Before—the lawn was bare and neighbors could stare.

Plant to Screen Your Window

Time and again the picture window performs only the function of allowing the neighbors to see into your living room. While you may not have anything to hide, it's a bit ridiculous to be constantly on stage to even the casual passerby. Pulling the shades seems to be a contradiction to the picture window idea so that's out. What can a home owner do?

Plants with color and character help screen the window without shutting off the entire view. The design of the walk, the variety of plantings will help to keep your neighbors more interested in the garden than in you.

In the photo, the heaviest screen element is the group of Australian flax *(Phormium tenax)* planted far enough out to look well from the windows. Contrasting with them are groups of European white birch *(Betula pendula alba)* which stay light and airy. Clusters of blue and white agapanthus (left) and the gray-foliaged dusty miller with yellow flowers (foreground) complete the planting.

After—attractive flower beds intrigue and greenery screens.

A Garden
for a Contemporary House

This is a garden for a modern house in Santa Barbara which recalls the simplicity and scale of classic European gardens. Yet, the only immigrants are the four Italian maidens who were given one-way tickets from Florence to their present abode. Silhouetted against the trees and mountains, they contribute to the strength and interest of the composition. (Try blocking them out and see how lonely the whole garden becomes.)

While perhaps this isn't a scheme many of us can have, it does illustrate several important points in garden design. It is often true that an exciting view or powerful background needs a compelling accent in the foreground to give depth and yet provide a means of relating back to the people who are there to enjoy it. Certainly it goes without saying that a mean dimension looks that much meaner placed against a great panorama and so the scale of the terrace becomes more important than the material from which it is built or the uses it is put to. While the swimming pool is very simple it is decorative all year long and rests easily in the garden set in a quiet and spacious terrace.

Designed for Pardee Erdman, Santa Barbara, Calif.

The four statuesque Italian maidens add strength and interest to this garden.

Go in League with Ivy

Vine patterns on walls may be done with many vines, but in San Francisco, where it can be dark, windy or both, the ivies become one of the surest, fastest and most easily maintained materials. There are over 100 varieties in cultivation.

They vary from the heavy growth of English ivy *(Hedera helix)*, and Algerian ivy *(Hedera canariensis)* to the slower growing and less rampant Hahn's ivy and its many variations in leaf size and shape. Some of the best known varieties are: California, Glacier, Pedata, Maple Queen and Needle Point.

All come in variegated forms. There is the even slower growing but rewarding Irish ivy with a long pointed leaf and an excellent variegated form, *Hedera hibernica*.

All varieties of ivy have but one thought in mind—to completely cover whatever they are growing on. This means that occasional care and training is essential. They may harbor snails and become infested with caterpillars, so some maintenance is required.

Nevertheless, for fast coverage, for year-in, year-out green, for either sun or shade and under all conditions from excellent to marginal, there is an ivy for every purpose.

*Green Algerian ivy has been stripped to let the trunks
make the pattern, with the foliage at the top of the fence.*

Designed for Mrs. Thomas Church, San Francisco

*Hahn's ivy trained on wire. The pattern was complete in two
growing seasons. It was six years old when the picture was taken.*

Designed for Mr. & Mrs. Arthur Stockstrom, Kirkwood, Mo.

Plant It Away

Too much enthusiasm in planting at the base of a house can do a garden in quicker than anything else. It is a shame to veil any house in shrubbery and sinful when the house itself is well designed. To heavily fringe such a house with foundation planting is to deny its architectural entity and to negate the strength it gives to the garden composition. The relationship between house and garden is maintained and emphasized by light, air and visual space as it flows freely from one to the other.

Restraint in planting and enthusiasm in its maintenance is the alternative. This approach may result in using an occasional plant to soften the house outline but still permit it to be positively stated by paving all along its base. With most of the planting moved further out into the garden, it can also be enjoyed from inside the house and the home will make its full contribution to the garden composition.

architecture is of interest, don't hide it with plants.

Designed for Mr. & Mrs. P. L. Menefee, Yamhill, Oregon

*Accent planting is the best way to introduce greenery and to
create a pleasing relationship between the house and the garden.*

Desgined for Mr. & Mrs. Corydon Wagner, Tacoma, Wash.

Make It Geometric

No one can deny the perfection of the French chateau garden as its hedges twist and turn in an endless variation of classic patterns called *parterres*. *Parterres* are first an overall geometric design, resting calmly in a designated space. Closer observation reveals a rhythmic play of squares and circles, cubes, spheres and spirals combining into intricate patterns.

Parterres are intriguing; they hold the viewer's interest as he mentally traces the curves, remembering perhaps his old geometry lessons. If one has developed an aesthetic awareness, he will be excited by the relationships of forms which the designer has established. If one is only beginning to realize these subtleties, he will find *parterres* fascinating, without realizing why.

Here at home, we return to our European heritage in planning our gardens and often recall these *parterres*. On a modest scale, they are suitable to our half-a-day-a-week (or less) gardening help. They are, in fact, ideal for this kind of care. Bi-annual pruning will maintain their form and good looks. Usually of evergreen materials—the greens of boxwood and euonymus or the grays of santolina and teucrium—they are suitable to our local climatic conditions. California is, indeed, a far cry from Chateau de Champs, but the similarity in the sweep of a hedge is as close as your property line.

Complicated in appearance, the precision of the design and the carefully pruned look can be accomplished with a minimum of care and effort.

Designed for Sterling Edwards, Burlingame, Calif.

*A well-ordered terrace provides the ideal setting for
budding Bernhardts, sylvan brides and garden party hostesses.*

A Terrace for Thespians

Do you have a budding Bernhardt or Barrymore among your children? If "the show must go on" and you have room in your garden, an outdoor theater provides entertainment all the year. Between performances, it may serve as a garden terrace, or may be filled with flowers, statuary or fountains. It is, of necessity, neat, formal and well-maintained.

The space is perfect for a luncheon party since it is like a room. It is equally compatible to a garden party since it is a garden. And, of course, it is an obvious spot to stage a wedding.

When not in use for something special, it is a calm and self-contained focal point in the garden. It is exciting or quiet, depending on your mood, and satisfying to either need.

Hedging's a Good Bet

Crisp, controlled hedges add strength and style to a garden, but only if they're the right scale and properly placed.

For the patient gardener, there's a long list of hedge material which time and care will develop into structural horizontals of green. The impatient can install a frame of chain link fencing at whatever height he wants his hedge to be and plant ivy. In several growing seasons the framework is covered and the desired effect is achieved.

The choice will depend on the color and texture he wants the hedge to be, his budget and his patience — or lack of it.

Many people say, "don't give me hedges that have to be clipped all the time." Actually, most hedges can be maintained in half a day two or three times a year. Can you keep your informal plantings within bounds in less time than that?

Designed for Mr. & Mrs. William Corbus, Menlo Park, Calif.

Controlled hedges can solve an infinite number of landscaping problems from a need for privacy to adding textural and structural interest.

Multiply Your Hedges

The traditional method of providing privacy from the street has always been the planting of a hedge. Probably a million miles of privet surround the interminable small properties of this country. California privet, *Ligustrum ovalifolium* (native of Japan), is equaled only by Pfitzer juniper as the most universally used plant in the world.

This privet's range is from three to twelve feet in height. A variety, *Ligustrum lodense,* may be kept at 18 inches while another Japanese privet, *Ligustrum japonicum,* will grow to 30 feet. It has a variegated form which is unattractive, and a golden form which is eye-catching and which, in shade, takes on a very pleasing chartreuse color.

The photograph below illustrates the use of a double hedge along a sidewalk, a device to provide elbow room, and is recommended when a sense of space is required instead of the abruptness of the hedge rising directly from the edge of the walk. In this case, the high hedge is privet and the low hedge is *Pittosporum tobira variegata.* Both are constantly and carefully clipped and should only be attempted when you are willing to spend the time to assure a well-tailored look. In the photo above, the French use alternating green and golden privet as a design in the Tuileries gardens, Paris.

Designed for Mr. & Mrs. Brooks Walker, San Francisco

*It is not necessary to use a single variety of
privet in the construction of a hedge; mix them
and tier them to create a more opulent border.*

*A successful hedge is a year-round green fence,
can be a separator of areas, a screen against the house
next door, a stage setting for flowers and a wind screen.*

Designed for Mr. & Mrs. Everett Turner, Modesto, Calif.

27

Create a Calm Composition

Putting anything as large and unyielding as a swimming pool between the house and a distant view can easily create a confusing picture. But with certain considerations in the design concept, a pool can fit calmly into a site without becoming a distraction.

Placing it in relation to, rather than in competition with, a strong element of the house is the first step toward creating a calm composition. The direction of the long axis of the pool influences the total effect. At right angles to the house, its length logically leads the eye to the great beyond while a pool placed parallel to the house and a view may become a visual barrier by the repetition of horizontal lines.

A continuous step below the coping drops the water level of this pool well below the terrace, creating an added shadow pattern and implying that it is a garden pool which may be used for swimming. An open metal railing allows the meadow to be seen from the house. A quiet paving complements rather than confuses the dramatic view.

The ultimate goal of a garden design is that it appear inevitable.

The "inevitable" garden design—all lines point to the view.

Picking Your Plants

A California gardener has at his disposal one of the largest selections of broad-leaved evergreen shrubs and conifers in the world, but with the availability of desirable plantings comes a basic problem: Which variety shall he plant? And how many?

Because there is so much to choose from, the eager planter is often tempted to use too many varieties too close together, leaving too little time to be spent on developing the full potential of any single plant.

By their shape, color and foliage texture, plants show that they are intended to enhance architecture, not hide it. One plant well chosen can improve a composition, where ten—fighting for light and air—more often result in utter confusion.

In these pictures, single plants have been given an opportunity to prove what they can do.

Don't be profuse when planting around your home. These photos indicate how minimal planting can enhance an architectural setting without engulfing it.

*The span of the arbor
links the hillside
cut with the rest
of the architecture.
A well-planned path
and careful planting
complete the scene.*

Designed for Mr. & Mrs. Paul L. Fahrney, Kent Woodlands, Calif.

Bridge the Gap

Too often—on a sloping site— the house is left facing a steeply cut bank wishing that it weren't there. This leaves the owner in a quandary—and in the middle.

If the cut was inevitable, there are the usual answers of planting the slope to control erosion, building retaining walls and terracing. But none of these solutions has a sense of togetherness which happens when some architectural element of the house reaches to the hill. This can be accomplished by a wall of the house or a fence disappearing into the hill, a bridge spanning from the second story to the upper level of the cut, a deck from the upper level resting on the slope, or (as in this instance) an arbor spanning the open space between the house and the cut.

The arbor makes the creatively planted slope a part of the house complex and makes a pleasant patio area.

Designed for Mr. & Mrs. Paul Wattis, San Francisco

Design
Provides the Answer
to Complex Demands

A small garden may have to mean all things to all people. Consider a family whose various members could not agree on how to include all their desires in a 35x40-foot city back yard. The problem becomes clear when you learn that one wants a broad redwood deck on which to relax and entertain large groups of people, while another wants a quiet Oriental garden. A third has no demands other than to ask that a rare and exciting old buckeye be given a worthy setting.

All wanted complete privacy from adjoining yards. That's an impossible challenge when neighbors tower over the garden, but a sense of privacy may be achieved by a garden's design.

While the resulting scheme is not a purist's delight, it does answer the problems presented by the clients. It also satisfies the requirement of the garden itself, which needed a counterbalance to the almost overpowering strength of the great tree. The structure, bridging the pool, gives the needed secondary focal point, and invites the deck people to take a short walk to see the sculpture.

The demands of three points of view are achieved through planning.

Be Bold in Design

Timidity in garden design is never more clearly shown than when you reach the edge of a precipice. The feeling that you must stop there shatters the proportions of the open spaces, leaves the house looking as though it is about to tip over the brink, and never affords you that pleasure of being out far enough to look back at your own house.

The addition of this semi-circular terrace denies any timid compromise with the slope. It seems to be reaching out for an oak tree growing in the canyon, and provides a serene, integrated composition with the house which could not otherwise exist.

Perched on its rise, the house appeared uncomfortable.

If you are on the edge of a precipice, don't be timid, terrace it.
The garden you save and beautify may be your own.

Designed for Mrs. Alexander Albert, San Francisco

Forced perspective used effectively in a French courtyard.

The Illusion of Space

Make believe is always appealing and to the designer, who is often faced with a small garden wishing it were twice as large, it's a fine trick of the trade. Various means of creating an illusion of space have been used, depending upon the century and the country in which the gardens were built.

The French call their solution *trompe l'oeil*, and during the Seventeenth and Eighteenth Centuries they developed this technique in gardens by using and combining trellis work, mirrors, painted murals, foreshortened paths and vistas. Under their capable hands, a flat wall enclosing an oppressive space became an invitation to leave the house and enjoy the out-of-doors. It promise was difficult to resist.

John Evelyn, in 1642, describes a well-painted perspective as "a very agreeable deceit" and Humphrey Repton, writing in 1795, says, "Nor is the imagination so fastidious as to take offense at any well-supported deception, even after the want of reality is discovered."

Such false perspectives can compensate for the restrictions of small city gardens, wherever they are. Illustrated here is a San Francisco garden which had negative assets: Cramped areas, dense shadows, towering neighbors and cold drafts. The French doors opened onto only 9½ feet of property. Center of interest was a depressing view of the neighbor's kitchen door.

By using *trompe l'oeil* lattice on a new wall, the neighbor's door has disappeared, his house has receded and the garden has visually increased. New center of interest is the sculpture by the late Adaline Kent.

38

Clever trellis design gives an illusion of distance to this flat surface.

Scale in garden sculpture is importa
to be seen, but not so large tha

Pick a Spot for Sculpture

Sculpture is one of the most pleasant man-made additions we can use in our gardens. It can be modern, a copy of an Oriental goddess or an Italian maiden newly escaped from the harem of a Renaissance garden.

In garden design, either may come first—the setting for the sculpture you already have, or a piece of sculpture to complete the niche designed as a point of interest in the garden.

If you are buying garden sculpture, the scale, the mood and your income will influence your choice. Whatever you select, it should be something you like and it should belong in the setting created for it. Very often, incidental sculpture—not always in view from the main rooms of the house—is more satisfying. If you have to walk a bit and turn your head to see it, you will have introduced an element of constant surprise and pleasure. You may not tire of it over the years as can happen when sculpture is continually in view.

Careful evaluation will tell you whether sculpture in the garden is for you or not. Some gardens simply don't ask for it. If you want it anyway, use it carefully, display it proudly and with finesse.

40

should be large enough
...rshadows your plantings.

Designed for Mr. & Mrs. Christian De Guigne, Hillsborough, Calif.

Designed for Mr. & Mrs. Gordon Packard, Atherton, Calif.

Sculpture can increase
the pleasure you receive
from your garden.

41

Desgined for Mr. & Mrs. Corydon Wagner, Tacoma, Wash.

Art, framed by foliage or an arbor, appears pleasantly outlined.

*The easily tended
planting areas of
General and Mrs.
Paul Berrigan grow
lush with flowers
during most spring
and summer months.*

Twin Gazebos
in a Formal Garden

By San Francisco standards, particularly in the Russian Hill area, the
Berrigan back yard was large, but that made it all the more frustrat-
ing. With all that space, sunshine from the east, south and west and
a specimen pepper tree, it wasn't really usable—the planting areas
weren't level and the cobblestone-edged paths plodded up the slope
with no direction in mind but "up."

General Berrigan, home from the wars, had a campaign in mind
—he wanted to fight the war of the roses on his own home ground
and on the level. Mrs. Berrigan was in agreement so long as the garden was decorative as well as productive.

Reorganized into terraces for flowers and planting, the new garden
is a symmetrical scheme which now steps up the hill with a definite

43

Latticed gazebos punctuate the symmetrical elegance of this garden.

objective—to get to a small plot of grass, twin gazebos and a rose garden on the upper terrace. The gazebos provide entertainment areas and are decorative year-round features when viewed from the house, and they invite the Berrigans and their guests into the garden .

The realization that the end can justify the means led the General to do battle with the cliff above. From the overlook he built at the top, he can ignore television antennae, enjoy the great north view of the bay or admire his roses.

For less-hardy souls, the latticed gazebos, silhouetted against the hill, add sustaining interest to the main terrace. The cobblestones were put to good use in retaining walls, wooden balustrades were used as railings and added to the second-story porch of the house; and the garden light, once a street lamp in Copenhagen, has a beautifully detailed copper hood.

44

The latticed gazebo invites the guests into the garden.

A Secluded Roof Top Haven

Dr. and Mrs. Richard Gratton were fortunate and they knew it. They owned one of San Francisco's most charming houses—built in 1904 and theirs since 1955. It overlooked the forest green-belt of the Presidio. In the distance, the bay sparkled by day and its bridges glittered at night. Something real and basic was missing from their over-all design for living, however—they wanted to grow green things of their own. They longed to *feel* the sunshine as well as see it glisten on the bay. Their yearning for direct contact with nature became increasingly important.

Since the house and property were the same size, they considered the only empty space left—a small 20 x 23 foot portion of a rooftop reached by a stairway from the third-floor studio. It wasn't much to look at and it sloped, but it had their cherished view plus lots of wonderful fresh air. They were sure it could be transformed into the usable retreat for which they longed. They admired Japanese gardens and the rooftop site seemed to offer one of those rare situations where a Western garden might visually reveal these influences without negating the philosophy behind them.

As completed, redwood platforms relate in spirit to the weathered shingle house. Natural forms and materials predominate. The everyday world is excluded by partial screening and dwarf conifers. Since the area is small, there was less room than usual for mistakes. Visual and usable spaces were carefully evaluated and temptations to introduce clutter were resisted.

To enliven the understated pattern of the redwood surfaces, Mrs. Gratton introduced decorative tea service and bowls. Instead of flowers, she substituted bright cotton cushions made of Japanese futon covering. Refreshments, per se, are limited to whatever may be easily carried from the kitchen three flights below, but this fits in with their original need. They wanted to partake of nature in plain air, and this they do—gardening a little more, but relaxing a lot more.

Designed for Dr. & Mrs. Richard Gratton, San Francisco

Two forms of sculpture were used. Boulders of feather-rock compose a design element, breaking the severity of the top platform. Tibetan figure supplies scale needed to relate small area to the large view. Shadows in the niche and under the platform lighten visual weight.

47

Look Down and Plan

How do you look from above? More and more people are flying these days, which means that more and more people are looking down on your country estate (if you have one). While airline passengers are not likely to drop in on you (you hope), they are definitely looking you over.

The design and proportions of your home in relationship to surrounding planting, drives and lawn become quite apparent when viewed from above. The shape of your pool, the color of your bikini and the lushness of your flower border all show from this elevation.

If your place makes a pleasant impression, in a design sense, from the air, the chances are the arrangement will be a pleasant one to live, work and play in when you are earthbound.

Designed for Mr. & Mrs. Sam Zall, Marysville, Calif.

2

Remodeling the Old Garden

As we suggested earlier, many people do not get the opportunity to start their gardens from scratch. Even if you're building a home, the expense of that operation (and it gets steeper every year) may prohibit you from thinking of the garden in the same unified terms. It can come "after we're set tled." And then inertia sets in, and the garden you moved into (and hated) is the same garden you move away from a dozen years later.

And most people don't even have the option of building the garden as they build the house. The house they moved into was inherited from somebody else—and Somebody Else is notorious for letting his garden go to seed or putting gnomes under toadstools or erecting huge ugly edifices which block the light and view. In any case, Somebody Else's tastes and requirements in gardens rarely match yours. So from the minute you move in you're uncomfortable in half your home—the outdoor part. And the adventure and the terror of moving needs no added problems.

All of which emphatically does not mean that all is lost. Far from it. As was touched on in Part 1, and as will be hammered home here, there are no insoluble problems. Nothing is hopeless. That old garden can be remodeled, and whatever its principal defect (and that must be carefully analyzed—there is nothing worse than solving the wrong problem), it can be corrected—with time, work and imagination.

Perhaps the best examples of the lesson that nothing is hopeless (we told you it was going to be hammered home) are found in "Victorian Remodeled", "Rural Remodeling" and "Create an Oasis From A Shunned Site." It is unlikely that you will have a problem as severe as that of the "Shunned Site"; it should therefore be encouraging that its owners were able to find a solution which fit their needs.

Some of the rest of Part 2 is designed to help you define your problem. It is possible that you are one of those who *know* your garden is all wrong but have been unable to figure out why. If so, many of the examples make suggestions on the nature of the problem and the method of solution. Perhaps it's the fact that your house doesn't match your garden, and it could be improved by a graceful transition from one to the other ("You Can Supply the Missing Link" and "The Gracious Transition") or just by changing the way the house looks ("Try a Lattice for a New Facade").

Maybe the garden is too bright ("A Way to Cool the Hot Sun"), or perhaps there's just a big ugly something that can't be moved ("Operation Transformation"). Maybe there doesn't seem to be enough space to work with ("If Your Driveway Dips, Focus on the Facade"), or perhaps your home is quite simply being smothered ("Remodeling for Additional Garden Space").

Whatever the problem is (and yours may very well not be among those listed), the object lesson for your own garden is clear. In the words of the Salvation Army, Garden Division: Everything Can Be Saved. Or to put it another way, for the third and concluding time: Nothing Is Hopeless.

*A garden that becomes
part of the house and
a house that moves
easily and gracefully
into the garden is
the ideal balance
for which to aim.*

Designed for Mr. & Mrs. Kenneth Van Strum, Hillsborough, Calif.

The Gracious Transition

Garden and house belong together, visually and actually.

The transition from one to the other should be gracious, and as effortless as the terrain will allow.

It should be safe enough so you don't wish you'd worn your duck hunting boots, and level enough so you don't spill your lemonade.

In the "before" picture, you see the steps which originally provided the only access to the lawn.

Added were a small terrace and (on the other side) an easy winding stair leading to the lower garden.

Before—distinctly separated and uninviting.

*The garden area was formerly
debris-littered and unappealing.*

Backyard Treasures
in a New Garden

One of the rewards of buying an old house is the unexpected pleasure of uncovering the treasures which may be buried in the garden.
As you first look at the backyard, it may look as though it has nothing to offer but a dozen loads of debris for the scavenger. The pros-
pect of getting it cleared suggests nothing but hard work. But once
you have your machete in hand, the jungle can be tamed and the
discoveries may be just what you need to give the new garden some
individuality.

Shingle facade of the home is a pleasant backdrop for this informal garden.

Hidden under overgrown bushes you may find only rusty bed-steads complete with mattress vines, tired jade plants, sad ivy and broken crockery. On the other hand, you may be like the Brooks Walkers and find a fortune in old trees, which money can't buy, full-grown boxwood hedges (not often available and always expensive), and urns, benches or sundials which have miraculously remained intact. These treasures were all used to develop the garden shown here.

Because it was also a south garden, they moved their living room to the back of the house so they could overlook it and enjoy its pattern, or reach it easily when they were in search of a quiet retreat.

You Can Supply
the Missing Link

There are frustrations in living in old houses which we can't over-
come, but seeing the gardens and not being able to reach them easily
needn't be among them. It isn't necessary to walk around the house
or through the laundry to reach the backyard. Windows are easily
changed into doors and most rooms can meet the garden, if the limits
of the property permit.

With typical old San Francisco houses, where the living rooms
are not at garden level, it's possible by various means. We can either
raise a deck to meet the new doorway or we can build a stairway
that leads directly to the garden. Decisive factors are the differential
in grade and the hurry you are in to get onto your terrace.

Behind either solution lies a basic principle. If we are to enjoy
our gardens, we must join them. They add to the pleasure of daily
living and anything that does that is worth the planning and the
expense.

Dining rooms and kitchens are traditionally connected inside the
house, often with a pantry between. Here is an example showing
them connected on the outside by way of a deck. Dining outdoors
and serving from the kitchen becomes effortless.

Linking the kitchen with the exterior deck is generally done as
a matter of course when building a new house. In remodeling an old
home, however, it can mean changing windows into doors and building the deck or terrace to fit the kitchen location. But everything is
worth it if you like to eat outdoors.

Before

*Redwood deck is only
a step away from
living room and
extends over to kitchen
for easy serving.
Privacy for deck and
flower garden is
supplied by fence which
screens city sidewalk.*

Designed for Mr. & Mrs. Charles Field, San Francisco

Reach
into the Garden

Many houses in San Francisco were built without any access to the backyard other than through the kitchen door. Instead, everyone looked through small windows down onto a handkerchief of grass banded in concrete with a flower-scalloped border.

Then houses, and people too, became less introspective. San Franciscans became aware of life down under. They learned that a garden could participate in entertaining and that even when it was too cold or windy to be in the garden, there was something pleasant in knowing that it was readily accessible. They started converting windows into doors and adding a simple flight of stairs to reach the garden easily and pleasantly.

They found that the garden responded to this attention by helping to soften the bad features of the house. Basement windows disappeared behind dados of green hedges. Blank bare walls became backgrounds for trees. Shadows played pleasantly on painted surfaces. Small gardens proved to be worth the effort.

56

Designed for Mr. & Mrs. Henry Sinton, San Francisco

The natural quality of a redwood stairway makes an easy transition from living room to lower garden terrace. Basement windows still have light but disappear behind boxwood hedge. New doorway is framed by flowering plum.

Intriguing Curves Enhance Small Backyard

There was nothing very wrong with the backyard of Mrs. F. D. Langdon, but nothing very right, either. Walks were angular and led nowhere in particular. The corner at the rear was overgrown and without character. We therefore replaced concrete with brick, laid in pleasing curves, and cleared out the back corner. This revealed the wall, which belongs to a neighbor and which has good "character." Just out of the camera range at the right is a patio that is covered by an arbor.

This steel frame sunshade was built out from the garage to provide shelter and an outdoor room.

These people needed shade and wanted privacy in a part of their back garden which was filled with a garage and shrubbery.

St. Francis, formerly sitting on the ground has been given the dignity of a niche.

Designed for Mrs. F. D. Langdon, Menlo Park, Calif.

59

Before: A veritable jungle greets the designer.

Create an Oasis
from a Shunned Site

Everyone used to shun the south side of this house. The sun beat down mercilessly. A small concrete terrace was too bright and reflected too much light. The chimney seemed large in relationship to its surroundings. The expanse of weeds was endless.

The area, however, was protected from the wind, the relationship between it and the living room and bedroom was good. And there was a pool in the owner's future.

"Eliminate the negative and accent the positive" seemed to be the order of the day.

So, a wood deck-terrace was built at floor level to kill the concrete's glare. A pavilion detached from the house provided shade and forced the outsized chimney into a more proper scale.

A terrace now juts into the pool, defining a wading area, yet leaving plenty of room for swimming.

Surrounded by grass and flowering trees, this once-shunned backyard has now become an oasis—the entertainment and leisure center for the owners.

After: What a difference planning can accomplish.

The uninteresting facade of this house was decidedly in need of attention.

Try a Lattice for a New Facade

If you buy an old house and the facade lacks distinction and charm, there's no doubt that you could improve its appearance by regrouping the windows, installing sliding sash, or adding a porch. However, such remodeling is expensive and the results may fail to justify the costs involved.

Another approach to the problem is shown here. When the present owners bought the house and handed us this problem, it seemed hopeless. But we decided to try.

The central section, with small panel windows and French doors, had a pleasing quality. It was left intact and painted white to make it stand out, while the bedroom and service wings, including the trim, were painted gray to make them recede. A lattice of redwood was built free of the house to line up with the rafters at the edge of the overhang. Painted white, softened by a tracery of vines, the lattice dominates, while the uninteresting fenestration of the wings disappears into the shadows. The space between the house and lattice allows for air circulation, window washing and vine trimming.

With the house unified, the garden space was developed as a formal terrace to include paving and a circular swimming pool.

Designed for Almaden Wineries, Paicenes, Calif.

An effective new look achieved with a latticed wall and a new focal point of interest.

Remodeling for
Additional Garden Space

An old house in Pacific Heights was smothered by an overgrown swarm of horticultural specimens that was almost impenetrable. It was decided to cut through this jungle and discover the valuable material that could be salvaged in a new garden design. Trees were pruned and trimmed and some new plant material was introduced. Since privacy was most sought after, the high line of trees was left in the background.

Even in a limited space of 40 x 40 feet, it was possible to provide strolling walks, save a small space for the cultivation of annuals and perennials and a formal greenhouse became a sunroom for looking at the garden on windy days.

Bright flowers in the sunshine and light-colored sculpture in the deep shade of the pines bring vitality to the new garden and as

64

This garden proves that a lot can be done in a small space.

viewed from the second-story bedroom it may entice you for a stroll through it's tiny world of trees, plants, rock and bright-colored flowers even before breakfast. Or without putting your foot into it you can do quite a bit of exploring just by looking.

A small courtyard was created in the front of the old house by construction of masonry walls, and a double gate with decorative grill opens onto the sidewalk. The large ferns soften the gravel and give an exotic character to the entry.

The old entranceway seemed too casual and cluttered.

Expand Toward the Street

There's a treasure in that small area between the house and the street, granted you can provide access and privacy.

Before, this house and its windows, a humpty-dumpty kind of step and an untidy front lawn were exposed to the street which was 16 feet away.

Now, a brick wall insures privacy from the sidewalk. A row of trimmed plane trees cuts out the view from the neighbor's second-story windows across the street and a pleasant, quiet sheltered garden is the result. New doors and wide steps provide access from the house. The entrance from the street is formalized and now looks as if it belongs to the aristocratic home.

The garden is now used often for eating, drinking, entertaining or simply for quiet meditation and relaxation. On a small-scaled city lot you must make the most of what open area you've got and in many cases there's much more there than you think.

Now the appearance is formal and uniformly neat.

Designed for Mr. & Mrs. Jerd Sullivan, San Francisco

*Surrounded by a high white wall and tall plane trees, this quiet, private
and well ordered Shangri-La now lies snugly between house and street.*

67

Operation Transformation

Here is the transformation of a backyard that not only converts a pasture-like area into a pleasant living-playing center, but also accomplishes a more pleasant scale for the existing out-size chimney.

The builder of this home left a large and bulky chimney, complete with barbecue on the outside, for the owner to cope with and explain, for it was far out of proportion with the rest of the building.

To solve the problem, a long but light arbor was built out from the house. It provides shade and pattern and brings the chimney into better scale in the composition by cutting it in half. The large terrace partitions the former "pasture," providing an ample entertainment area as well as play space for the children. There is still room at the perimeter for a lawn and plantings.

Before—The outsize chimney dwarfs its surroundings.

*After—A lattice places the chimney bulk in its proper
perspective. Paving and benches partition the area.*

Before: Dilapidation but basically good design.

Rural Remodeling

The good design of this old farm house was as obvious as its state of dilapidation and it was rewarding to recapture its original charm. It was even more interesting to add an ambiance that never existed before; as part of a large ranch, the house had not been in a garden setting.

However, the owners bought the ranch for a comfortable country place suitable for raising their children as well as Black Angus cattle. Along with the house remodeling, a new fieldstone wall was built to support a terrace of generous proportions. It is used for entertaining large groups and overlooks a wide sweep of lawn which rolls down to the pool.

The new garden is easy and relaxed and results in a pleasant rural setting for both the old house and the new owners.

*After: The pool, carefully groomed lawn, plantings
and reconstruction make this a show place.*

Bricks
Warm a Garden Space

San Franciscans grasp at any level sunny spot they can find and develop it as usable garden space.

This house had some valuable land with a southern exposure going to waste along the street. It had a dining room which lacked privacy from passersby and a nicely detailed entrance which needed accenting.

A brick wall, painted to match the house trim, defines a small dining terrace and shelters it from the wind. Red brick paving adds warmth to the garden and keeps the construction materials unified—an important consideration in a small space. Guests are led from the entrance court to the front door by a series of wide platforms—a more inviting approach and easier to navigate than a single flight of steps.

The trimmed rubber trees (*Ficus nitida*) take the San Francisco wind as they add height to the screening of the wall. The juniper (*Juniperus sabina tamariscifolia*) is a year-round base for the trees.

A line of rubber trees—
behind them, a brick wall
and behind it,
a small dining terrace.

Entrance court,
in platforms.

In 1933, a sad house in need of repair.

Victorian Remodeled

Saving the Victorian beauty of early San Francisco houses can be quite expensive. Yet, if the owner enjoys the style, remodeling can be a labor of love. And today, the latest conveniences can be installed behind mouldings and panels for more modern living.

The home shown above was built in 1862 and was ready for destruction when first remodeling began in 1933. Since that time continued restoration, with additional Victorian architectural embellishment, appears to have recaptured all of the majesty we generally associate with homes of the period.

A new garden with a curvilinear walk (foreground) provides a pleasant entry and setting to enjoy the symmetry of the house facade.

*In 1965, restored and mellowed by a mature garden it seems
proud of its origins.*

*The walk from the street to the house winds thru an informal
garden of ferns & shade plants.*

3

Landscaping the Entrance

It is a cliche that first impressions are important. Every job applicant, for instance, is told that the impression he makes in the first 10 seconds of an interview will go a long way toward determining whether he gets the job.

The condition of his haircut, the polish on his shoes, the set of his shoulders, even the color and pattern of his tie, are frequently considered indicators of his character. These things together create a kind of code, and the job applicant hopes the message conveyed is something like: "I'm a sober, mature, responsible, eminently employable person, well worth whatever salary I might ask, a stable family man and a credit to the firm."

A house has the same kind of code. Most people want their house to say something like: "You are welcome here. The people inside are cordial, open, friendly people, of impeccable taste and unimpeachable manners, with (as you can see) a fine eye for color, texture and line and a deep appreciation of beauty." And what makes that impression, what transmits that code, is, overwhelmingly, the entrance. It is the entrance, which your guests see for a fleeting moment of a visit which may last hours, which says much about your house and, by extension, you.

This does not mean your house should necessarily attempt to sidle up to people and ingratiate itself (nobody likes a pushy house), or be so staid and bland that no one could possibly be offended. But it should reflect the kind of person you are and the kind of impression you want to make. Entrances are for people as much as the rest of your garden .—ideally, your entrance should serve both you (to give an amiable first impression) and your guests (to make them comfortable and eager to continue with their visit).

Our first example ("Give Your Entrance Grace") reminds us that, in making the entrance a place of welcome, simplicity and harmony are the most important ingredients. It also emphasizes an obvious but strangely overlooked fact: In simplest terms, your entrance should be designed to show where your front door is. If people occasionally tap on your side door or crunch through your flower beds because they took a wrong turn somewhere and have lost themselves near the service yard, perhaps a little landscaping is indicated.

"A Front Door Should Say 'Welcome' " and "A New Court of Arrival" point out that even if your entrance is far away from the parking area, design can make the path to your door, graceful and obvious. "Welcome Mat" and "Red Carpet Psychology" remind us of another important function of the entrance way: It must be suitable for conveying guests from A to B in style—that is, it must be wide enough so that visitors can walk side by side and stand at the entrance waiting for you to answer the doorbell without slipping off into the ivy, and it must make the guests feel welcome and comfortable while they're walking and waiting.

And of course, a great entrance can make a home—and a great entrance is possible no matter where the house is. For city dwellers, a fine entrance ("Why Share Your Front?") can make a house distinct from its drabber neighbors and brighten up a whole street.

In short, then, your entrance is the world's first impression of you. And if the world wouldn't hire you for a job on the basis of your entrance, perhaps it's time for a change.

Give Your Entrance Grace

"Through these portals pass the happiest guests . . ."

Can you say this about the people who must get from their parked automobile to your hearthside?

Is the path they must take as mysterious as a London fog and filled with as many hazards? Do new guests tap timidly at the side or back door and say, "I'm so sorry, but I thought this was the entrance."

Do they have to play a game of mental hopscotch over a conglomeration of asphalt, concrete, brick, flagging and terrazzo before arriving at the comparative safety of the entrance hall? Are there the

Designed for Mrs. Paul Kelly, Santa Rosa, Calif.

The importance of the entrance cannot be overemphasized.
Its expansiveness functions as the proverbial red carpet to your guests.
Here the curves lead you unerringly to the front door.

added hazards of teetering stepping stones, overlapping junipers, sudden turns and unexpected steps to face before they can grasp the knocker?

You can make the few obvious repairs. You can prune the lilac that slaps them in the face and the barberry that rips their nylons. You can light the steps and put a sign saying "service" pointing to the back door. But only by thoughtful planning can you contrive to make the guest feel he has arrived in one piece and is welcome.

If the evening is to be successful, it must be a pleasure to arrive. How to do this involves a study of the physical needs and the psychological aspects of the process of entering.

The great paved courtyards of the Renaissance palaces were not for convenience only. When you drove into one, you knew you had arrived. You could see the main entrance and were sheltered by the architecture. You could relax. The only remaining thing to do was to step across the threshold, and that, too, was a pleasure.

The automobile is here to stay in the foreseeable future and must be dealt with logically in our planning and accepted as an asset in our visual scheme. Man and his automobile may be compared to the man and his horse of other years. They seem inseparable. They arrive at a destination together. The guest should feel a sense of welcome while he is still in his car. He should be led inevitably to his destination, be able to park with ease and then alight in a recognizable composition where his next move is obvious and effortless.

The next move is to the front door, but here is where we most often fail to maintain the excitement of arriving. The area is cramped, covered with vines or overgrown with shrubbery. It's often only a few feet wide and seldom sheltered from the elements. Your guests must enter in single file. Only one can mount the steps to ring the bell, and he has to back down again to open the screen door.

The arriving guest should be standing in one of the most important areas of the total composition of your property. A narrow path, a step and a stoop don't begin to solve the problem. The space in front of the door should be generous in size, properly scaled to the house and designed with some grace and elegance. You are making an important impression here. So are your guests. They deserve a stage with appropriate backdrops.

Designed for Mr. & Mrs. Jack Euphrat, Atherton, Calif.

The "stoop" and its steps have been moved thirty feet out to the driveway to provide a continuous red carpet to the front door.

Designed for Mr. & Mrs. Roy Robinette, Menlo Park, Calif.

Welcome Mat

Give your guests plenty of elbow room outside the front door or garden gate so they may feel they have arrived before they push the bell. Let them enjoy the planting, the architecture, the paving patterns in an area scaled to their anticipation of the hospitality just over the threshold.

When a platform is small, there is a feeling of stinginess about the space which may reflect on the owners of the house as well as dim the delights of being a very important guest. A few extra square feet

Designed for Mrs. D. G. Bennett, Redwood City, Calif.

A front entrance should never be hidden from view, or small and cramped.

of space outside the front door give a graciousness to the whole experience of being a guest which more than compensates for the additional cost.

Guests will also appreciate an expansive landing as they leave. They like being able to say good-bye in a relaxed fashion before they face the steps down to the parking area and the hazards that await them on the drive home.

A New Court of Arrival

The front door to this remodelled house was 80 feet from where the guests were to park their cars. Unless they were skillfully led to it by the design of the garden, they could have found frustration long before they sighted the front entry.

To ease the journey from car to canape, the welcome usually stated by the front door is given to the garden entrance.

Stucco screen walls are pierced by an entrance gate of wrought iron to allow a glimpse of the paved garden court. (This immediately suggests that something interesting is beyond.) Spanning it is a redwood canopy—expansive in scale—suggestive of warmth and hospitality, its front columns resting on fieldstone piers which flank a broad inviting stairway.

The arbor, simpler in detail after its opening statement, continues to the front door. It is logical to follow it to the entrance to the house. En route, the arbor reaches for an old wisteria that existed and adds interest to the dull facade of the house, gives a sense of shelter to the court and puts shadow pattern on the paving below.

Before the magnificent redwoods were thinned, there was a straggly garden area beneath them where only darkness prevailed. Now, light and sunshine filter down onto a shaded terrace of red brick. The vista back to the redwoods is nostalgic as one waits in a quiet garden court for the front door to open.

*The garden gate gives the welcome
usually extended by the front door.*

Designed for Mr. & Mrs. E. M. Ricker, Hillsborough, Calif.

*The arbor leads the way to the front door,
and adds interest to a dull facade.*

Red Carpet Psychology

Designed

The moment of arrival at your front door should be a memorable experience for your guests. The setting should make them feel important. It may be calm or exciting, but it must say that the host realizes that this is a special occasion. It is the psychology of the red carpet.

I went to lunch last year in Baltimore where there was not only a real red carpet flung down the steps, but a Bear flag was flying from a small standard. In the attic of this home there are the flags of all the States. While this was a highly personalized gimmick, it left no doubt but we were expected, important and welcome.

The V.I.P. treatment can be suggested simply by a generous amount of space around the front door, or by the volume of air in which you stand before ringing the bell, or the pot of flowers you look at, or the kind of knob you reach for. (Why do so many people have chimes?) If the steps have just been swept and the pots just watered, it is obvious that the hostess is in a tizzy of anticipation and can't wait for you to arrive.

So, now—fling open the front door! Do you see tantalizing vistas of further areas to explore? Or do you see a claustrophobic space, too small and too dark, with too little light and too many unexplained doors?

Here, then, is something really important: Don't drop the ball as your guest crosses the threshold. Both sides of the front door must say welcome, must be spacious, must remain an effortless and pleasant continuity from driveway to hearthside to highball.

Sharpen your pencil and cut down or rearrange your space to fit your budget, but still let your entrance hall have the size and quality of the mansion you dreamed of building. No economies effected can make it worthwhile to walk·from an entrance garden into a telephone booth.

& Mrs. Bernard Ford, Hillsborough, Calif.

Your entrance should give every guest the VIP treatment.

Designed for Mr. & Mrs. Edward Eyre, Woodside, Calif.

Designed for William Hume, San Francisco

After: Seclusion and unity are gained by walling in the forecourt.
The facade of the house now joins an inviting entrance walk.

Why Share Your Entrance

When you step off the sidewalk and enter your home grounds you should have the feeling that it's your own private world. Why be saddled with inadequate planting? Why be chagrined because your neighbor's drive flanks your walk? Why be annoyed by the lack of privacy in your front yard?

There are solutions to these problems. A little expense and a great deal of planning are necessary, to be sure, but worth it in the long run. Take the town house shown here.

This home now has a quiet, secluded entrance garden. The formal facade is recognized and accented by moving the entrance to the center. The wall alleviates the confusion once created by the juxtaposition of the house next door. The over-age yew trees have been retired (to a country lane, we hope) and replaced here with round-headed *pittosporum undulatum* (victoria box). Most of all, the composition has assumed the quiet dignity befitting a town house.

Before: A hodgepodge frontage.

88

4

Fences, Screens and Stairs

The three things mentioned in the title are not the most glamorous aspects of making or remaking a garden. They are, perhaps, the most pedestrian and commonplace of the arrows in the designer's quiver. Anything with two levels of any kind requires the consideration of stairs; anything that needs to be separated requires consideration of a fence; anything that needs to be protected requires consideration of a screen. Every yard has at least one of these things; many have all three.

It would, admittedly, be nicer if we didn't have to think about these things and could worry exclusively about majestic trees, bright sprays of flowers and deep cool pools, but fences and stairs are the backbone of any garden. Their placement and design is often the first problem, and upon the solution to that problem often hangs the fate of the entire garden.

This part is roughly divided between examples devoted to fences and screens, and those devoted to stairs. "Out of the Wind and Into the Sun" and "Fence with a Purpose" remind us that form depends on function—first decide what you want the fence *for,* and that will help you decide what kind of fence you want.

"Raise Your Beds" and "Train a Vine for Privacy", by contrast, deal with the obvious, overwhelming problem with any fence or screen: The darn thing is so abrupt. Since the human eye somehow considers open, unencumbered vistas the grandest and most pleasing of sights, anything that starts by destroying open vistas has two strikes against it. But the eye can be fooled, or at least mollified, and these two examples present some suggestions.

Stairs (or steps) start with no such handicap. The human eye, for the most part, enjoys stairs. Psychologists say that, in dreams, stairs symbolize an invitation to the most pleasant and enduring of man's activities. So the problem with stairs is not to pretend that they are not there when they are (as with fences), but making them work with the rest of the garden while still fulfilling their primary objective—taking people quickly and comfortably from one level to the next.

There are very few rules which cannot be broken with delightful results, but here's a vital one with regard to stairs: Twice the riser plus the tread equals 26 inches. If, for instance, the grade dictates five-inch risers, the tread should be 16 inches (five inches plus five inches plus 16 inches equals 26 inches). For an eight-inch riser, the tread should be 10 inches (eight inches plus eight inches . . . you get the idea).

The step should have a pitch of about a quarter inch to allow for drainage. For the rest, it depends on the environment. Shape, for instance, is determined by the kind of garden the steps are going into, and the materials are determined by the owners preference and the overall pallete being used in constructing the garden.

Ivy topper adds privacy with exuberance.

Designed for Floyd Gerow, Palo Alto, Calif.

Train a Vine for Privacy

Most communities regulate the height of boundary fences. Six feet is just enough to let the lights of neighboring windows shine in your face, or their clothes lines distract from your more relaxed moments. This is a bad height for appearance's sake but the limitation exists.

On the other hand, there is no restriction on the height of plants. Therefore, "screen planting" is a must in most closely built-up neighborhoods.

Illustrated here—in an area too narrow for heavy shrubbery—is variegated Algerian ivy trained to the top of a six-foot fence. By its own exuberance it piled up several feet above the fence in no time. Community regulations are thereby circumvented and privacy insured for the suburbanites.

Before—Six feet is a good height for a man, but awkward for a fence.

Designed for Mr. & Mrs. Jack Euphrat, Atherton, Calif.

A fence directs attention like a frame on a painting.

Fence with a Purpose

There are all kinds of fences. The choice for your garden—either solid or open—depends entirely on what goes on behind it. Obviously, a service yard is better left unseen and solid fences will hide cluttered areas. If you want a psychological division of the garden space, or if you want a frame of reference for an intensely developed area or a space dedicated to a special purpose, an open fence is the answer. Not only will it punctuate that section deserving special attention, but it doesn't shut off the view of whatever part of the garden lies beyond.

Designed for Mr. & Mrs. H. C. Blackwood, Menlo Park, Calif.

To distinguish areas of planting . . .

Designed for Alice Irving, Santa Barbara, Calif.

or to establish a point of reference.

Do Fence Me In

A problem which confronts many an owner of a contemporary home is the relation of the house to the street, particularly when that is the best orientation for garden living. Sometimes this is not controllable either because of regulation or property boundaries.

The home pictured here had such a problem. When the house was completed the owners found that their living room with its expansive glass walls faced the street and was exposed to the view of all passersby and to neighbors across the street. A six-foot sapling fence was the solution. By continuing the terrace area as a wooden platform, to save filling around the trees, a protected entertainment area was created. It is shaded during the day, and lighted at night, and nobody knows it's there.

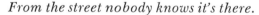

From the street nobody knows it's there.

From inside, the picket fence encloses the view,
focusing attention on the garden.
Building a deck through and around the trees
makes a pleasant, informal entertainment area.

Raise Your Beds

A garden can be easier to look at, as well as to maintain, if certain planting areas are raised above the main grade. If you have a high retaining wall or fence and want to reduce its visual impact, a raised bed at the base will do miracles. Your eye will subtract the lower level from the over-all vertical height and negate the problem.

A flat lot may need this subtlety as well as a hillside, which may demand it.

If pulling a weed or plucking a flower is a chore at ground level, a raised bed can halve the strain and double your pleasure.

Designed for Mr. & Mrs. Charles S. Salzenstein, Peoria, Ill.

Designed for Mr. & Mrs. John L. Bradley, Hillsborough, Calif.

*The three
raised flowerbeds
shown here
are different but
perform the same
function of negating
the abrupt walls.*

97

Designed for Mr. & Mrs. Guy Witter, Pasadena, Calif.

A pleasant way to hide the ragged plants of fall and winter.

Screen a Seasonal Garden

Vegetable and cutting gardens are great assets to the garden but it is impossible to keep them at the prime of visual perfection throughout the year. Vegetables and flowers have seasons and can look ragged as they begin to fade into the long dormant winter. The last rose of summer deserves credit for perseverance, but may not add much to the view from the terrace.

The objective of this design was to screen the beds from the terrace, yet not put them in a high-walled compound of their own. A series of baffled walls lets them be a part of the garden, yet not constantly in view.

Baffled by a vegetable or cutting garden out of season?
Baffle walls hide a multitude of vegetation.

Glass around the patio . . . an inviting extension of the house.

Out of the Wind and into the Sun

The sunniest spot in a garden may also be the windiest and, as every designer knows, that's a tough combination to beat. Wind is tricky and fickle—protecting a sun pocket from it is neither simple nor sure.

However, a wind screen of glass can help to a great extent—it magnifies the sun's intensity and sitting near it is like turning up the thermostat. Being transparent, there's no feeling of claustrophobia—nor the frustration of not enjoying all there is to see beyond it.

When glass is combined with the same materials as the house, the resulting windbreak can be a harmonious note in the composition.

Glass for poolside warmth . . . and evening wind protection.

Steps to Separate

Retaining walls tend to separate areas in a garden, but sometimes the designer wants to minimize existing differences between levels. Often he prefers the areas to flow together as an expanse for ease of use and visual effect.

Broad steps used as a retaining element instead of a vertical wall can solve the problem. With steps, there is no reason for a railing to separate the areas further. With steps, there is no need to worry about extra chairs for party seating.

The most important consideration is the riser-tread relationship. Only cellar steps can have steep and stingy dimensions and a broad flight, in particular, must have gracious proportions.

Rome can get away with the Spanish Steps, but the domestic-scaled garden can't cope with broad flights of more than half a dozen steps. They are an exceedingly strong design element, but properly related to the over-all scheme, their dominance adds interest and unity to the garden.

From terrace to lawn, with love.

Designed for Mr. & Mrs. Austin Earl, Atherton

Brick

Designed for Mr. & Mrs. R. E. Hills, Atherton, Calif.

A broad flight with just a few steps allows the areas to flow together.

Choose your materials to make a graceful transition between different levels.

Designed for Mr. & Mrs. Richard Hoefer, Bronxville, N.Y.

Stone

The Naturalness of Stone

Mexico has many delightful old outside stairways that are integral parts of the high walls they climb. The steps are steep, and there are no railings for the timid; but they add strength, pattern and interest to the practical need of getting up and down. Obviously, the demands of safety engineers and law suits were not problems for the conquistadors.

On a more modest scale, the same stairways work very well in our gardens. They allow for access to an upper terrace without destroying the beauty of the wall itself when viewed from the lower garden.

One may ignore railings when the change in grade is no more than four and a half feet, and the steps shown here feel perfectly safe to their owners. All they require is a little caution, and that is always a good idea anyway, isn't it?

Designed for Mr. & Mrs. Stanley Barrows, San Francisco

*Steps in the garden,
made of natural rock,
introduce variety of
form to a retaining
wall and allow access
to upper terraces.*

Designed for Mr. & Mrs. William Wallace, San Francisco

105

Make Them Natural

The character of a garden stairway is determined to a great extent by the material used in its construction.

When the designer wants a "natural-looking" flight of steps, as opposed to a frankly formal and architectural one, he thinks of stone as it occurs in nature—water-worn or weathered, warm in color and with a possible patina of lichen. He knows that such stone collaborates with the mason's skill in creating a stairway in sympathy with its surroundings.

Since stone is a natural complement for plants, their use in the stairway itself heightens the recall of a natural scene. Pockets of topsoil, provided while the steps are being built, assure proper growing conditions. Planning ahead is important, but doesn't have to be obvious in the final effect. Plants soften a stairway when used along each side. The texture of the foliage contrasts with the surface of stone and each is enhanced by the comparison.

Designed for Mr. & Mrs. Roy Robinette, Atherton, Calif.

The basic idea: Create contrast in the composition.

Upgrading with Steps

When a broad flight of steps can also retain a change in grade, the question of whether they should be curved or straight may come up.

There is no rule to determine this other than the overall garden design. It's a matter of creating contrast in the composition. A curve seems more so if it is contrasted by the strength of a straight line. The interplay of curving and linear forms adds zest to the pattern. It is the prerogative of the designer to decide where the emphasis should be placed.

Once the question of design is settled, there are practical precedents as to materials. Brick or stone, being modular, is easy for building curved flights. A straight run may be of brick, stone, concrete or wood. The choice again reverts back to the need for using materials harmonious with each other, with the architecture and with the mood of the garden.

Designed for Richard Duff, Kentfield, Calif.

The interplay of curving and linear forms adds zest.

Brick

Stone

Wood

Designed for Mr. & Mrs. Paul Fahrney, Kent Woodlands, Calif.

Up and Down With Redwood

The obvious material to use for steps going up a rocky hillside is more rock. Nine times out of ten it works and in three designs out of four it is the most logical material. Yet sometimes an all-stone garden can become monotonous and stone masonry can overwhelm the viewer by its own weight.

To avoid this pitfall these steps were constructed of redwood planking. Each tread is made of two 3 x 6s. They provide a soft, lightweight material, a regular cadence in contrast to the stone and the deepest shadow in the composition.

5

Trees

Somehow, as soon as anyone begins to write about trees—and this seems to happen whether the article is horticultural, architectural, botanical or even industrial—some fragment of Joyce Kilmer's poem wanders unbidden into the text. But trees deserve better than that. We might remember what Heywood C. Broun, the pudgy, tough-talking journalist, said about it: " 'Trees' (if I have the name right) is one of the most annoying pieces of verse within my knowledge . . . "

There are, of course, many bits of fine writing about trees, and generations of poets and philosophers have attempted to capture their special fascination for man. But perhaps the finest tribute to the necessity of trees to the human spirit is the simple admonishment by Carl Linnaeus, the father of modern botany: "If a tree dies, plant another in its place."

Trees, after all, are one of the most impressive and majestic elements a landscape architect can work with. They should always be treated with respect. Trees are the hardest to place, partly because they are also the hardest to remove. But they can also transform a home or yard, give shade and fruit and color, dignify the ordinary, provide natural perspective and give the whole garden a loftier purpose.

For this reason, you should always make very sure that the tree you were thinking of removing cannot in fact be saved. After all, it took nature anywhere from 10 to 300 years to get that tree in its current shape; you should carefully consider before you kill it in 20 minutes. "Screen with a Natural Stand" reminds us to consider pruning before chopping down; it is possible to both keep the tree and reveal the view it supposedly hides.

On the other hand, some trees have got to go. It's sad, but there it is. The most important thing is still the total home and garden environment; whether it's a comfortable and enjoyable environment as well as a beautiful one. The aesthetic combination of form and function is still the governing factor. If a tree is choking your house or yard, by all means get rid of it (see "Don't Spare That Tree").

Trees, for that matter, have their own function: They give shade. The ideal backyard has both sun and shade, which more or less means that the ideal backyard has a tree in it—other solutions to the shade problem are generally much less satisfactory. "Is There Both Sun and Shade on Your Terrace?" and "Pierce the Paving with Trees" are examples of how to use trees for maximum effect.

Perhaps the most interesting and significant lesson about trees can be found in "A Tree Makes the New Look Old". It is important—and heartening—to realize what trees do for their surroundings. Because trees have such a feeling of permanence, such a natural stability, everything around them looks more natural, in tune with the landscape and the world. The right trees provide instant serenity—something, in this modern world, which cannot be cherished too highly.

Designed for Mr. & Mrs. Frederick Murphy, Atherton, Calif.

Screen
With a Natural Stand

Lifting the foliage line of trees by pruning their lower branches changes the role they play in the garden composition.

As screening along property lines or for hiding an untended area, the lower and thicker they are, the better. But other gardens may need more light, or a terrace under the trees, or a feeling of expanse, or all of these, as was the case with this garden.

The day for pruning dawned bright and clear and the axe was sharpened in anticipation. Soon, the light filtered in from behind the redwoods and the cleared space, now available, became an inviting spot.

The backlighting of the grove was an added reward and should exist even on a gray day. This was achieved by using golden bamboo as a low screen behind the new tanbark terrace. Its highlighting adds drama to the tree trunks and a year-round gaiety to the green garden.

115

A Tree Makes the New Look Old

Unlike people, gardens never strive for perpetual youth—they want to look old from the day they were born. Their greatest beauty comes with maturity. New gardens try to look old before their time. They are in luck when old trees exist to help them out—even one tree of scale and stature will give a garden a semblance of middle age before its first birthday.

However, to both the designer and garden lover, certain species, regardless of size, come as mixed blessings. The native California bay shown here was such a tree. If it were to survive civilization in the new garden, certain long-acquired habits would have to be respected. Being used to winter rains and summer drought, it wouldn't tolerate a lot of water, while paving too close to its trunk would stifle the root system.

If the owner were to cherish it, rather than chop it down within six months, certain faults would have to be accepted and coped with. All evergreen trees shed a few leaves a day for exercise, but a bay tree excels in being difficult. It fights captivity, has messy flowers, drips oil, welcomes pests and disease and is unfriendly to other plants if they get too near.

A redwood platform—octagon shaped and 26 feet across—was chosen as the design element most sympathetic to these limitations. It reflects and increases the tree's dominance, is visually pleasant, is used as a garden seat or buffet, and has even been a bandstand for music at a party, and a terrace on which a bride and groom cut the cake.

On the practical side, the deck allows for controlled watering of the tree and permits air to reach its roots—the paving stops just inside the shadow line. The leaves and their inevitable stain blend with the dark wood while grass and other plantings keep a safe distance.

Yet, without this one old tree, difficult as it was to please, the garden would have an entirely different feeling. It would take many years to approach the character pictured here, photographed after a sweeping, but before it was two years old.

Designed for Mr. & Mrs. Gordon Packard, Los Altos, Calif.

Serene and majestic in its domination of this recreation area,
the old California bay tree adds maturity to a newly created garden.

Don't Spare That Tree

Yesterday's houses were high off the ground, needing a buffer of lilacs to relate them to the garden. Today, they are low and friendly, sitting at ground level. The foundation has disappeared but the habit of planting to hide it still remains.

Heavy foundation planting is probably the result of looking at your completed house and feeling that it seems to be stark naked. You rush to a nursery and buy as many plants of every size, shape and color, including forest trees, as you can afford.

You place them neatly around the house, sigh with satisfaction and move in. Several years later, you are fighting to liberate the windows, tunneling through the aborvitae to get to the front door and attempting to club the forest trees into submission.

The garden of Mr. and Mrs. A. C. Helmholz of Lafayette had that smothered feeling. Rooms became dark at noon and frustrated guests began appearing at the side door. After a major clearing job, they have recaptured those forgotten but rapturous moments when they saw their house for the first time standing sturdily on its own foundation.

*With its unsightly, excess
padding of overgrown bushes
and trees sheared away,
this charming house appears
to be years younger than before.*

Designed for Mr. & Mrs. A. C. Helmholz, Lafayette, Calif.

Before: A tree worth saving.

Save That Tree

Never underestimate the value of a handsome tree. Protect it, build your house and garden compositions around it, for it offers you shade, shadow, pattern against the sky, protection over your house, a ceiling over your terrace.

Its situation and structure may determine where the house will be built and decide on the size and shape it will take. Its shade permits what is otherwise folly—placing windows into the glare of a western sun.

It can also, as in the instance shown, provide an enviable example of living sculpture.

*After: Framed by the surrounding house and
brick patio, the tree becomes living sculpture.*

A tree offers you shade and protection, grace and strength.
Be very reluctant to deprive your yard of its beauty.
Sometimes a tree needs a little help if it is to be saved. It
does so much for you; you can surely give it some support.

Designed for Mr. & Mrs. John E. Hawkins, Atherton, Calif.

Trees relieve an otherwise bleak, concrete approach.

Pierce the Paving with Trees

A bare house, approached by bleak paving, can repel guests rather than attract them. On a hot day, the glare may seem intentional.

One or two trees, arching over an ample entrance, can change the whole effect, and the front door can become inviting. The roof line may become more interesting if interrupted by tree pattern, and the suggestion of shade will soften the paving.

You gain by planting trees without losing the virtues of adequate paving which is easily maintained.

Is There _Both_ Sun and Shade on Your Terrace?

It's one thing to have a sunny terrace on one side of the house and a shady terrace on the other. It's better to have your sun and shade on the _same_ terrace.

Nobody likes to pick up chairs, cushions, ping pong table and drinks and move from one place to the other.

Your terrace should be large enough so you can move in and out of shade on the _same_ terrace. Besides, in any group of people you will find some who prefer shade and some who prefer sun, and others who want to sit with their feet in the sun and their heads in the shade.

If there is a large tree nearby, build your terrace out to it. Even if it seems far away, reach out for it. It will give your garden better scale. Remember it's nice to sit near the house and look at the garden, but it's also pleasant to sit out in the garden and look back at the house. If there isn't a big tree near the house, plant trees in the terrace or build arbors and sun shades over it. Plant them so they will shade only a part of the terrace.

It's ideal to have both sun and shade on the same terrace.

Designed for Mr. & Mrs. Richard Rheem, Orinda, Calif.

An unbroken expanse of lawn can be transfigured
by trees—transplanted full-sized.

Replant the Forest Primeval

A sweeping lawn shaded by large live oaks is an irresistible idea to most of us. Under certain circumstances it can happen overnight.

The oaks shown in the photo above were boxed and moved full-sized from an area to make way for a dam. They were placed and studied until the composition seemed right and then lowered to within 18 inches of the existing grade. Topsoil for the lawn was then filled in to the grade of the trees.

Within a few weeks, this open field at the entrance to a country place became an oak-studded lawn.

6
Swimming Pools

All gardens are, in one way or another, attempts to recreate artificially what nature has, in other places and in other combinations, created all by itself. In the artificial situation, however, man can control the natural elements so that they can best be appreciated and lived with. In some cases, that means taking things that are already there—like trees—and using them. More often, it means importing things that mother nature forgot.

Like water. Very few homes are blessed with either a year-round lake or a year-round stream. The water must therefore be pumped in, and it must run or stand in an artificial bed. Since streams are impractical, both in terms of initial cost and of upkeep, that leaves us with artificial lakes. In other words, swimming pools.

At least, that's what we'll call them. How much swimming can be done in them is up to the owner. If he and his family are of an athletic bent, and if he lives in a sunny part of the world, he'll probably want a practical swimming pool, with accessible dressing rooms, easy maintenance and accessories designed for life around the pool. Others may want to appreciate the pool from afar. In that case, we can sacrifice the convenience of the swimmer in order to enhance the view of the observer.

A tour through the various levels of this idea is provided in the first several examples of this part. "Are You Going to Build a Pool?" shows a selection of pools from one end of the spectrum—all of them designed primarily for swimming and swimmers. The idea here is that the pool-for-swimming pool can still be that familiar old rectangular shape and still be attractive.

One step further away from strict functionalism gets us to a European-style villa pool ("Viva The Villa"), which gives this Italianate home a measure of grace, beauty and depth it had not previously enjoyed. One more move, and we arrive at "The Garden Pool" and a pool obviously never intended to be swum in, but to add highlight and emphasis to the garden.

Finally, high formalism. As can be seen in "Formal Pool for a Deep Plunger", this can only be done in a yard of generous dimensions (by an owner whose pocketbook is equally generous), and it was the size of yard that determined this exercise in geometrical serenity—not at all useful but (we think) very handsome.

Later examples are reminders that pools are not restricted to big lots or ordinary shapes. A pool can wander anywhere in the yard (The Shapes of Pools"), and a pool can enhance even the smallest city yard (A Pool in a Limited Space"). Indeed, the city yard can give us one of the most successful multi-purpose pools. In "The City's Formal Pools", we see a formal, elegant pool which is also a perfectly fine swimming pool, and all this in the heart of the city!

As we have seen, pools are another useful tool in the landscape designer's kit—a far more versatile and useful tool than most people imagine.

Designed for Mr. & Mrs. Kenneth Van Strum, Hillsborough, Calif.

Before the Digging Starts

The first question any prospective swimming pool owner must ask himself is: Is the fun of a swimming pool worth the initial cost and considerable upkeep involved, as well as the responsibilities inherent in a purchase of this magnitude? Once a swimming pool is installed in a backyard, it's hard to trade it in for a lawn again.

Assuming that you've decided that a swimming pool is in fact right for your yard, the question arises: Is your yard right for a swimming pool? Will it fit on the site without too many grade problems? Can the drainage problem of the pool decking be properly solved? Is there enough sun? Is there too much wind? Is there enough flat space left over for paved sunbathing and furniture areas? Is there room for adequate dressing and bathroom facilities to be included nearby? Can you serve the inevitable Cokes and hot dogs

Designed for Mr. & Mrs. Dewey Donnell, Sonoma, Calif.

A free form with an island.

easily without upsetting the house routine, or will you build a structure for poolside activities? Are you ready and able—as undoubtedly will be necessary—to double or triple the initial pool contract costs to provide these amenities?

In one case, the problem was space, as it often is on a hillside lot. It was decided that a small, semi-ornamental pool would fit best in the area, and the owners agreed that it would suit their needs. If they had wanted an Olympic-sized extravaganza, however, they would have had to forget the pool idea entirely or move to another location.

In another, the problem was clearly not space; it was that the suitable site was some distance from the house. That little cabana on the right solved most of the problems, but please remember: That little cabana on the right doubled the initial pool installation cost.

Designed for Mr. & Mrs. Thornton Howell, Santa Barbara

A 24 foot circle on a steep cliff.

Designed for Mr. & Mrs. Fred McCrae, Sonoma, Calif.

A rectangle on a natural hillside far from the house.

131

The Classic Swimming Pool

The questions of the size and shape of the pool and surrounding areas need thought and coordination before the hole is dug. Being the largest single design element in the composition, the pool cannot be hidden or disregarded on properties of an acre or less. Its success or failure, esthetically, will depend on where it is placed, what forms are chosen as being most sympathetic to the site, what materials will do the most to heighten possible dramatic effects and blend most harmoniously with the house and the distant landscape. If the whole garden area is to become primarily a swimming club for your family and friends, the influence of the pool and its surroundings will involve the house and terraces in its scope and activity and will reach to the property lines.

Most clients request a pool which will be convenient and useful and so conceived as to look well the year round within a larger design concept. Often the designer finds that the standard rectangular or classic forms are not to his liking, and he strikes out into the exciting (but dangerous) area of curved, angular or non-objective art forms. Many, dictated by the available space and contours of the site and informed by a knowledge of scale and proportion, are highly successful. Others, through ignorance or over-enthusiasm, become distinctly hysterical.

So there is much to be said for the simple, classic swimming pool. A good example would be the Jerd Sullivan pool in Saratoga, California. There is nothing particularly fancy about the pool or the deck around it (the cabana has its points of interest), yet it suits the purposes of the family and lends grace and simplicity to the terrace below the house.

The simple, rectangle fits best in these surroundings.

133

Variations of the Theme

Just as there are people for whom the swimming pool is the navel of their lives, there are people for whom a swimming pool is just a secondary appurtenance. For them, odd and interesting designs are more suitable. The Bradley pool is halfway between useful and ornamental—a pool which is functional for swimming yet more interesting and serene than a standard pool. The other pool wraps around the master bedroom, with its three-quarters-of-a-pie shape, and takes advantage of the only flat area on the property.

A few reminders: A pool of any shape can have underwater seats to add to the enjoyment of lazy or indifferent swimmers. They allow for a cooling-off period, free of exuberant children splashing in the shallow water.

And, no matter what size or shape your pool takes, be sure that thought is given to the coping, the tile and adjacent paving. There are times when the pool coping should not be accented but appear to be a continuation of the paving. Another design will need contrast to give a punch line to the design. Pool tile, used only to prevent stains on the plaster when the water line fluctuates, need not be blue. It is a misconception that the water looks blue because of the tile—ever since Hiawatha's time, it's been the sky that does it. Your pool will appear larger and more elegant if the tile is a neutral color —tan, say, to match the coping, or gray to suggest shadow.

Designed for Mr. & Mrs. John Bradley, San Mateo, Calif.

Designed for Dr. & Mrs. Hugh David Phillips, Atherton, Calif.

Why Not a Terrace in the Pool?

If you are planning a new swimming pool, a terrace is a must, unless you long for a simple body of water surrounded by grass, and are willing to accept chlorine damage to grass and have no place to put furniture.

If, for any reason, you feel like being different, build a tongue of it out into the pool, but keep that tenuous connection to dry land. You'll want to watch the children on one side and the swimmers on the other. You will want to pass lemonade down to guests who are already wet and at the same time you will want to keep your hand steady and your feet dry.

A peninsula into the pool, whether a circle (as here) or as a free form in a less formal setting, will answer all these needs.

A terrace serves many purposes.

Designed for Mr. & Mrs. William Wallace Mein, Jr., Woodside, Calif.

There was room here for a rectangular pool but the circular shape seems more at home in this pleasant sylvan setting.

The Shapes of Pools

There is no fixed rule about what shape a pool should be. It may be influenced by your own convictions and prejudices. It may be determined by how many children you have; how far they want to swim, and how deep they want to dive.

The pool shape could finally be chosen by how you want it to look in relation to the rest of the garden; how it composes with the immediate landscape and the distant view. Rectangles, circles, ovals, classic shapes and, very occasionally, a free form may all be possibilities when you begin to think about having a pool.

Illustrated here is an 18 x 42-foot rectangular pool in a formal setting and a 24-foot circular pool in a quiet hillside of trees. Neither of these would have looked as well in the other's setting.

In a flat, level area and where poolside space is plentiful a rectangular shape can be the best solution for your pool.

Designed for Mrs. Paul Kelly, Santa Rosa, Calif.

Designed for Mr. & Mrs. Donald Fritts, Burlingame, Calif.

Garden Pool for
a Dedicated Swimmer

More often than not today, a prospective swimming pool owner is concerned not alone with the pool's size and its function but with the visual impact on the total garden composition and the esthetics of its shape, color and material. This awareness of the importance of a swimming pool as an asset to the landscape has led to some experimentation by garden designers and considerable soul-searching by prospective owners.

For instance, in the pool illustrated, the wife wanted a pool in keeping with the simplicity and elegance of her traditional garden. So did the husband, but he is also a vigorous swimmer and did not wish to settle for a pool that would curb his enjoyment of the sport.

To satisfy this apparent conflict of interest, the form chosen was a quatrefoil design. Its derivation from early classic forms fits into the existing scene, and 40 feet of length in two directions keeps the swimmers happy.

For non-swimmers there are roses and the fabulous rhododendrons of the Northwest as well as a snack bar in an adjacent pavilion. Divers must be satisfied with jumping off the raised flower boxes, for a board and a ladder would have been foreign to this scene.

Designed for Mr. & Mrs. Corydon Wagner, Jr., Tacoma, Wash.

*A formal pool, symmetrical and elegant, that allows
plenty of exercise room for the swimmer.*

The arcs of the steps were used to determine the pool's structure, and now both blend harmoniously together.

Use What You Have

Many architects take the start-from-scratch approach when redesigning a backyard, but we usually try to blend the new harmoniously with the old. For instance: The curving steps existed at the Charles Thieriot home before the pool was installed. But note how the steps have been made part of the pool structure, and the arcs of the steps have been used to determine the shape of the pool. The symmetry of the garden is retained—and even enhanced—with the substitution of a pool for a stretch of lawn. And, as a bonus, the pool is still perfect for a moderate amount of swimming.

Before, a stretch of lawn.

*The symmetry of the garden is retained and enhanced by
the substitution of a pool for a stretch of lawn.*

Viva the Villa!

In the garden pavilion of the Villa Caprarola in Tuscany, sculpture shares equally with architecture and gardening to produce a perfect composition.

When the Christian de Guignes added a garden pavilion to their Italian house in Hillsborough, the architects borrowed much of the grace and perfect proportions which we associate with the Renaissance Italian villas. Also used were the large pots, sculpture and the classic coping on the swimming pool to reproduce—in a modern age —the simplicity, proportion and ease of maintenance we associate with these early gardens.

Designed for Mr. & Mrs. Christian De Guigne, Hillsborough, Calif.

*At Left: Caprarola, an inspirational source for the elegant
de Guigne Renaissance garden pavilion in Hillsborough shown above.*

Designed for Mrs. George Lyon, Burlingame, Calif.

A Pool
in Limited Space

Keeping up with the grandchildren by building a pool for their enjoyment is a new problem being faced by owners of many gracious old houses with charming gardens. This problem is compounded by the following: Where can a pool fit into the landscape where it will not spoil the original garden and still be far enough away to escape the shade and leaves from handsome old trees?

The pool designed for the Burlingame garden of Mrs. George Lyon is 14 x 34 feet, small but adequate for the family's enjoyment. It was positioned on an area formerly a flower garden. The garage is used as one side of the covered sitting area. Behind that are the filter and dressing rooms.

Interestingly enough, addition of a pool for the grandchildren often starts grandparents swimming as well. Of course, they inherit the problem of all pool owners: When to find the pool unoccupied in order to practice their side strokes.

*New brick steps and border
along outer edge of paving
reflect materials of
old house and garden.
Wood seating substitutes
for chairs and also covers
a continuous splash-drain.*

The City's Formal Pools

As recently as 15 years ago, the idea of having a private outdoor swimming pool in San Francisco would not have been taken seriously. Some have now been built, however, and with the water heated to a comfortable 75 degrees they can be used often enough to be worthwhile.

Of course, when they practically fill up the entire back yard, they must be designed as decorative garden pools with swimming as an added attraction. Obvious swimming pool accoutrements—ladder and diving board—are best omitted. Behind-the-scenes essentials—filter, heater and dressing rooms—should remain out of sight.

The 25 x 49-foot garden shown here has a 14 x 29-foot pool which ties in with the formal decor of a French town house. Centered on the dining room windows and just below the terrace-deck, it is an integral part of the composition which extends the theme of the house out into the garden. The pool can be enjoyed all through the year, even on a cold winter night. Its soft illumination adds an exciting sparkle and gaiety to the scene.

Designed for Mr. & Mrs. Edward Bodman, San Francisco

This pool was designed to complement a formal town house.

The Garden Pool

Garden pools mean hard work. Whether you're in the mood or not, they must be kept clean and planting should be well-groomed.

However, if you're willing and your garden is large enough to include a pool such as the one illustrated (an octagonal 20 x 20 feet), you might consider using water-worn stone as the material to define the form. Beautifully weathered and large in scale, such stone blends with other natural materials to create a quiet and restful composition.

The stones can be laid with topsoil joints so that planting may soften the lines. The fun is in deciding where moss and alpines will "occur" without obscuring the dominant strength of the form and the material used.

A tree close by will accent the pool and don't forget the value of the shadow it will cast. Near water, the reflection of pattern from tree trunks and foliage can be more meaningful than the tree itself.

A garden pool needs hard work to keep it well-groomed.

Designed for Mr. & Mrs. Ralph K. Davies, Woodside, Calif.

*The garden pool, lined with massive stones,
dominates this wide expanse of lawn. The shade tree
and the flowers between the rocks add interest.*

The Garden Pool *(continued)*

Designed for Mr. & Mrs. Wellington Henderson, Hillsborough, Calif.

A formal pool and fountain supplies the sound of water in a courtyard.

7

Decks and Yards

If they think about it all, most people think that decks are a new, primarily 20th Century, contribution to architecture, probably growing out of the Western way of life. But this is not, in fact, the case.

The wooden balconies of 18th Century European design were forerunners of the deck, and the spacious front porches and verandas of English and American architecture during the Victorian era were ancestors. But porches have become detached from houses and wander quite freely around the property—sometimes even jutting out over it, providing the illusion of level spaciousness on a sloping hillside lot. These kinds of wandering porches are what we call decks.

In this respect, decks (and, for that matter, their more attached forerunners) can be seen as attempts to bring the indoors outside, to bring the plush furniture, cleanliness and amenities of indoor living out into fresh air and unobstructed vistas of the outdoors; to combine, in other words, the best of both modes of living.

Decks are perhaps most useful as problem solvers, and it is amazing the variety of problems they can solve. As suggested above, a properly designed deck can transform a hillside lot (as in "The Advantages of Decks") and avoid that nagging feeling of horizontal claustrophobia. And decks can also be used (see, "Fly into Space on a Deck" and "Pavilion in the Tree Tops") to take advantage of other people's trees or to extend your living area beyond your own trees to take advantage of a view.

But decks can be used for far more purposes than just a wooden terrace helpful in exploiting hillside lots. They can also be used as the family's prime living area in the summer, as in ("A Deck for Living"). And, especially for the home owner on a budget, decks can serve as the ideal compromise ("A Reappraisal of the Back Yard"), using natural materials in an outdoor setting but retaining the low-maintenance attractions of concrete or asphalt yards.

So consider the deck. As the title of yet another example in this chapter indicates, decks are places where adults can levitate and meditate, a near-Oriental sanctuary in the tree tops.

The Advantages of Decks

As California's population grows it becomes harder every year to find land flat enough to hold our houses and automobiles while leaving space for our gardens. Sites that were considered impossible 15 years ago begin to seem choice as we see what is happening to the countryside—our hillsides having been led to the guillotine and converted into ledges on which only the mountain goat is at home.

Man finds it takes more than a bit of doing for him to make these shelves livable spaces. There are legal restrictions to please; physical set-backs imposed by daring cuts and fills to satisfy, and mental hazards to circumvent, namely "horizontal claustrophobia" or the feeling of being trapped by the monotony of a site that is uniformly too narrow throughout its length. It is costly, but possible, for him to rise above these problems to enjoy the amenities of his property.

His first attention must usually be given to preventing the hill above from sliding into the living room and this problem is most realistically solved by a retaining wall of wood, stone or concrete, depending on the height and nature of the cut.

On the down-hill side he has a choice. The first is to build another wall and fill behind it to create additional flat land. However, this can be unattractive—esthetically, practically and financially—for several reasons: Original grade on which to rest the wall footings may be buried under tons of earth; existing trees may be jeopardized by filling soil around their trunks or packing it tightly over their root systems, thereby shutting off air; and natural drainage must be redirected and carried in tile beyond the barrier of the wall.

The alternate solution, of course, is to build one or more decks depending upon the amount of additional space required for pleasurable outdoor living. With a deck, the dominant line of a fill may be broken (and consequently softened); the shade of a tree may be used in a sitting area, or the last hour of the sun may be relished; the house may be viewed from a decent distance so that it is seen in the full round instead of in profile; and the view, which was part of the sale, may be accented.

The deck shown was related to the existing trees so that one side is sunny when the other is a shade terrace. These decks are utilized as focal points from the house, allow a closer look at the view and relieve the monotony of the ledge.

Designed for Mr. & Mrs. Paul L. Fahrney, Kent Woodlands, Calif.

Decks are 2x6 redwood, resawn surface, stained to blend with
trees and countryside. Oaks are native to Marin hillside.
When the sliding doors are opened, this deck becomes as much
a part of daily living as any room in the house. It gives
the effect of tieing the house to the tree and land.

157

Easy access to the deck area is provided by the doorway at the left.

Citydweller's Deck

On many steep sites, gardens start outside the basement and are not convenient for outdoor living as they extend to retaining walls and/ or jump up to follow the slope of the original hill. The easiest way to bridge the gap—to provide garden space at the level of the second floor—is by a deck.

In the solution shown here, the light well needed by the lower floor was developed as a garden court around which the bridge-deck was designed. The bridge allows the court planting to be seen from the dining room and puts the sitting area where it and its furniture are apart from the house. The deck connects to a garden and serves as an intermediary link between it and the house.

Owners who want to view their back yard and use it, too, score on both counts with a functional, transitional garden deck.

Fly into Space on a Deck

Here is an unusual deck, but you can plan your own orbit into space. A deck can extend your patch of outdoors right into the view of forest or beach on a flat, maneuverable level.

On many Bay Area homesites hilly terrain makes a normal, flat, Midwestern-type lawn area an impossibility. To retain a sense of dignity (and an even keel) while entertaining or relaxing out of doors in these circumstances, a deck is a necessity. It can be cantilevered or mounted on posts but however it is accomplished, the view it provides can be exhilarating.

*The ground pattern of the
garden is seen from above.
The white band between the redwood
deck and the haydite covering
on the terrace is the top of
the concrete retaining wall built
along the original slope from which
the deck takes off into space.*

Designed for Mr. & Mrs. Justin Day, Sausalito, Calif.

*Since a railing would
have cut across the view,
a two-foot seat was used
at the edge of the deck.
This is high enough to create
a psychological barrier
which works for reasoning
adults. Temporary fencing
could be used when small
children are in the family.*

Tree Houses for Grown-Ups

Filling earth around trees on slopes to create flat terraces is inexcusable. Trees become sickly or die when the normal breathing and drainage is disturbed. Sooner or later, the sitting area is no longer under an inviting canopy of green. Of course, costly drainage and aeration may prevent such a calamity but why take a chance when decks offer a safe alternative?

Decks are at home among the tree trunks and people are happy when they are among trees. As with the garden shown here, a deck made it possible to enjoy a close relationship with the native oaks at the floor level of the house. And, most importantly, the lives of the trees are not endangered.

*Set off from the house, shaded and protected
by large oaks, this deck is a peaceful refuge.*

Pavilion in the Tree Tops

Civilization has moved us out of trees and into houses, yet the magic of life in the tree tops persists. As children, we find fascination in tree houses. As adults, we can recapture the mood by building decks high among their branches. So doing, we learn the fact that trees mean much more to us when we are close to them. The sky seems bluer when viewed through foliage and a vista has depth and perspective when framed by tree branches .

Tree-top living makes us realize how dull it can be to just look *at* trees instead of seeing *into* them. Trees are living sculpture—made by a pruning saw used with the proper proportions of caution and reckless abandon. Skillfully done, blobs of green can be transformed into invaluable art forms in a garden composition.

Living on a Sausalito hillside, Mr. and Mrs. Justin Day now look at their trees from a new angle. They look down from the second story to enjoy sculptured forms outlined by the view. The trees now embrace a garden that once was outer space.

On the deck they enjoy the way the trees arch above and around them. They like the way the foliage frames the harbor beyond. They appreciate being able to move into the deck's shade when the sun is too hot on the haydite or when they need shelter on a windy day.

These are all levels of experience which can heighten the pleasure of living on a wooded slope. If this were a fable instead of fact, perhaps the moral would be, "Don't reach for the stars, reach for your trees—and prune them."

Railing along deck on one side opens the views to a fern and camellia garden below. It also creates greater deck space.

The Problem—to enhance a large, flat garden area.

A Functional Feature
as Focal Point

A focal point in the garden can be decorative, as with sculpture in a lily pool, or it can be the most useful feature in the scheme.

The garden shown here, with a redwood deck as the dominant element, illustrates the latter principle. When the planning started, many solutions seemed possible because the space was open and uncomplicated with well-placed trees. However, the house floor was 15 inches above grade and schemes with all the sitting areas at ground level seemed dull as well as inconvenient. The plan lacked interest until the deck entered the composition.

By extending the floor level out into the garden, it becomes both a strong form in the design and a place to sit, easily served from inside. As an esthetic aid, the deck adds to the importance of the house, breaking the vertical separation between it and the garden below. (Foundation planting would have done just the reverse.) The shadow cast on the paving adds another dimension by relieving the

The Answer—an inviting and very livable patio.

flat expanse of concrete. Acting as an overlook, the deck is also the best place from which to view the pattern below.

The concrete terrace, in turn, was designed to accent the splayed shape of the deck in its role as the garden focal point. All the paving lines work together to increase its importance, although the curved form also invites guests to the front door.

It's not a place for an avid gardener since the planting areas are small and simply treated. Its advantage is that it would work for a busy family in Peoria, as well as for a family on the leisure-oriented coast of the Pacific.

Before

A redwood deck, projected from the house, dominates this garden and adds a dramatic design element to an otherwise drab area.

The problem: How to enhance a large, flat garden area, achieving a graceful transition between the house and the yard.

168

The solution: A redwood deck which breaks the monotony neatly and helps to bring the indoors out into the open.

After   Designed for Mr. & Mrs. William Sears, Santa Barbara, Calif.

Before

After   Designed for Mr. & Mrs. Dana De Hart, Hillsborough, Calif.

*Before, almost an eyesore
—a joy to no one.
The addition of a multi-level
deck brings easy access and
outdoor living to a city lot.*

A Reappraisal of the Back Yard

Only a few years ago the backyard of a city lot was not considered an asset. There was no access, no view, no place to sit and no plants except an array of unpruned roses and half-dead Christmas azaleas.

Love of fresh air and a search for sun instituted an agonizing reappraisal of the potential of the left-over space around a city house, and how to get to it from the proper rooms.

In this example the kitchen and breakfast room have been opened onto a wood deck at floor level and the living space extended over two-thirds of the rear property. There are still lots of plants, seen from a slightly raised elevation, and now there is plenty of space to sit and enjoy them.

After   Designed for Mr. & Mrs. John McGuire, San Francisco

171

Levitate and Meditate

Once, the area shown was a steep oak-studded hillside, far below the house, crossed by trails for the adventurous and perfect area for older children to play.

But what about younger children? This family needed a place where it could entertain on sunny days and where small children could play safely and still be watched.

The expanse of wood deck was the only sensible solution. A sturdy railing with small mesh fabric covering the center rail makes the deck safe for small children. The built-in bench reduces the amount of furniture needed when guests are entertained. The deck is located directly off the kitchen—convenient for both child-watching and food-serving.

But a deck can be more than that. It can be a tree house for adults, too.

Bridging from the house terrace, a redwood deck can float into the treetops, 20 feet above the ground and 40 feet into foilage, shade and shadow. There is a sense of levitation here that could only be duplicated by a space platform.

Here is a place for quiet contemplation, bird-watching, unhurried reading, and unparalleled views of the ferns and azaleas below.

Designed for Mr. & Mrs. Stephen D. Bechtel, Jr., Piedmont, Calif.

A place for contemplation, bird-watching, unhurried reading, or just gazing out at the hills and the sky—a treehouse for adults.

Designed for Mr. and Mrs. C. W. Miller, Corte Madera, Calif.

Designed for Mr. & Mrs. Lawrence Blair, San Francisco

Fake a Door

A problem facing many city dwellers with a small but precious space in the rear garden is the existence of a neighbor's garage on the property line.

To screen it with plants takes invaluable footage from an already restricted space. To plant trees may create shade where San Franciscans want sun.

On the theory that the neighbor never sees it anyway and— granting that he's co-operative—here is a solution which makes it seem really all yours.

Admittedly, the door is pure whimsy since it goes nowhere—but it might, and as such is an invitation to come onto its terrace.

New vertical siding, a few moldings and an old door from the wreckers, plus a brick terrace and appropriate plantings, have created the illusion of space, comfort and welcome.

Before, a neighbor's unsightly garage.

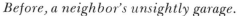

8

Storage and Work Areas

It would be nice (in a sense) if architects could design a garden without people. All kinds of lovely formal effects would be possible, and every corner of the yard could be used to maximum advantage. Then, presumably, people could stand on a small platform somewhere and admire it. But gardens are for people—for people to live in and work around as well as for them to gaze at, and all designing should take this into account.

Which brings us to storage and work areas. Almost every home has them, and in most homes they are just the poor stepsisters of the garden, hidden behind the garage or in some dark corner, a jumble of rakes and shovels, broken flower pots, a sagging cardboard box full of decaying leaves, a few half-mended toys and miscellaneous effluvia. This alleged work area is usually treated as though it didn't exist, and guests are always expected to ignore it and inspect the garden, pretending it isn't there. But it is visible, of course, and it is an eyesore. And it needn't be.

With a little organization and planning (a few shelves, perhaps, or a door or some brickwork), all that clutter could be put away and the space could become a useful and attractive work area. But the work space should be carefully designed to fit the person using it, or else it is organization to no purpose. In the same approximate amount of space, we can get such disparate work areas as those pictured in "The Problems of Gardeners", "Potting and Puttering" and "A Hobbyist's Garden" of this chapter.

And it is useful to remember that deceit is a weapon in the arsenal. Some things do look better hidden, but the hiding should be artful and pleasing. In a sense, the garden pictured in "Put Your Plants in a Bed" uses deceit, because the work area has been fragmented, with a little bit of it near each bed. And in "Use Walls to Store", a virtual labyrinth has been constructed to provide for an efficient working area.

We again see that livable gardens are not necessarily ugly gardens. There is no reason for anyone to tiptoe around his garden as if it were a Ming Dynasty vase. It is as silly to be afraid of designing a garden for the things you need as to be afraid of designing it for the things you like. Utility and beauty are not incompatible ideals.

Designed for Mr. & Mrs. Stuart Thompkins, San Francisco

Garden Workshop

The garden service area is a counterpart of the kitchen in a house. It's where all the magic that keeps the garden well-fed and healthy is stored.

This area need not be large and can be an attractive addition to any garden. Organization is all that's needed to provide the essentials —a work bench and storage for tools, topsoil, peat, fertilizers, sprays, flats, or flower pots. Its service to the garden is further increased if there's room for a few cut flowers and a "sick bay" for ailing plants.

Reserve some space for a work area before you give it all away to other garden activities. It will be invaluable to the well-being of the garden and increase your gardening pleasure.

177

Don't Show Clutter

Not this!

You don't have to accept service area clutter as part of the view even if your garden is very small. If you can't spare the room for a tool house and potting bench under cover, a garden fence will provide the opportunity to organize the confusion.

The fence doesn't have to be tall—even a low one will hide pot racks or a work table, while the space underneath can be a convenient place for empty pots, flats and garden miscellany.

A low fence won't visually constrict the garden—it will create a feeling of spaciousness by screening out the unsightly.

Counter space is as important here as in your kitchen, and if you can add cupboard and tool storage, so much the better.

Plan the area for what you have and keep it as neat as you would your house.

Or this!

Make your work area large enough for the work planned.

Racks against a fence help keep pots in their place.

A Decorative
Garden Work Area

If your property is large enough and you have the inclination and
energy, a work area and cutting garden can become a major feature
of your garden design. Since it's to be seen and admired by your
guests (don't you show off your modern kitchen with pride?), it
should be decorative as well as useful and must be well organized
with someone in the family neat enough to keep it that way.

A structure can combine tool storage, potting bench and general
work area as well as any other of your special requirements. Other
less attractive or bulky essentials such as manure pile, compost bins,
incinerator and greenhouse should be easily reached but not seen
from the flower garden.

Raised beds become year-round design elements, may be filled
with a miscellany of flowers suitable for cutting, vegetables, roses and
iris without destroying the unity of the plan and may be full or
empty without destroying the basic pattern.

Designed for Mr. & Mrs. Lee Johnson III, Fort Worth, Texas

The raised flower beds, in addition to their tidy appearance, save the gardener much bending and stooping and provide a place to sit down. The grass panel has a stabilizing influence in this garden. If you would rather have more growing space, it could be turned into more raised beds or filled with row after row of tall corn.

Use Walls to Store

Two things seem constant in the design of contemporary homes and gardens in Northern California. Walls are constantly used to screen garage turn-arounds and service areas from the rest of the home, and most houses today lack space for dry storage, tools and supplies.

By putting these two ideas together you can have a storage wall. The baffled walls shown here are three feet wide, are roofed, and together form 33 lineal feet of storage space.

This is equal to a room 10 feet square but is a much more efficient way to store tools and garden accessories than the cubicle.

Privacy (between the entranceway and the garden) is also assured even though wheelbarrows and people can pass from one area to the other without opening gates.

Devious are the labyrinthian ways of this garden screen.
And when the doors open, the screen reveals a plentiful supply
of always-needed room for tools, wheelbarrows and peat moss.
A path winds past storage areas back to a private patio.

A Hobbyist's Garden

Gardens need an accent to give them character and interest. Often the focal point of the area can reflect the owner's special hobby:

Here is a detailed photo of a metal arbor with a redwood slat roof designed over a pot stand. This was planned as a display area that still offered protection for the owner's potted plants. Hours of relaxing work are spent in the greenhouse and garden service area developing plants worthy of star billing and display.

It is a colorful spot. Broad wood steps lead to red-brown tanbark, a soft natural material used to contrast with the grassgreen of the lawn. The redwood fence of board and batten is stained alternately gray and black.

We see that the hobby area is functionally designed and isolated —the display area centrally located. This allows the owners to putter with pots and plants without disturbing the living areas of their home. Yet the better results of their work are seen by guests from the house and terrace.

Redwood steps blend with the green of the lawn

Put all your potted plant handiwork on one display rack for accent.

The Problems of Gardeners

We all know the undeniable charm of strolling down a garden path brilliant with annuals and winding through an informal garden filled with flowery surprises and delights. Gardens like this exist and dyed-in-the-wool gardeners are eager and willing to spend the time and care to maintain the casual and cluttered perfection this type of garden offers through the seasons.

Most of us, however, need a garden area which is always neat and ordered with a minimum of work. Sacrificed are the heady delights of dividing perennials in the fall, mulching the hibiscus for the winter and the thousand and one fascinating chores that need doing through the year.

The garden shown here (the latter type) has neat edges, crisp forms and permanent materials. There are some raised beds for cut flowers, roses and flowering trees, but emphasis is on a garden which will look good all year.

Too stiff and uninteresting for you? Then you're a true gardener and should have a lot more dirt to push around, and plenty of time to do it.

*Is your gardening time scarce, but your lawn
area large? Careful planning makes this garden
enjoyable with a minimum amount of upkeep.*

Potting
and Puttering

A down-to-earth gardener is an experimenter, a putterer and a collector. He can spend countless, happy hours making cuttings, trying out new sprays and speculating on the results of a new soil mix. These and all other activities of a garden work area can be pursued more fruitfully in a space that is conveniently planned. A work bench wide enough to hold flats, accessible storage for tools and miscellany, and potting soil close at hand are important considerations. Sun, shade and surfaces to hold cherished collections are also needed.

Whimsy entered this work area with the addition of an old bathtub, but it works very well for soaking newly potted plants and for certain spray jobs.

Each garden service area can express the user's own special interests and the way he likes to work. All it needs is thought in the planning stages.

*A place
for everything
and everything
in its place.*

Potting and Puttering (continued)

Designed for Mr. & Mrs. Robert Marble, Palo Alto, Calif.

The right place

9

Children's Play Areas

For years, gardens have been designed to give pleasure to adults, as if adults were the only people who lived in a garden. And, for years, it was not all that bad an idea—most of the people who had designable gardens were very wealthy indeed, and children could be relegated to another part of the estate entirely, only to be brought out at specified times accompanied by their keepers.

However, appealing as that way of life occasionally seems, it's as dead as the 50-cent haircut. Children have been integrated into the total life of the 20th Century family, and the space situation in the average home is such that the children's play area cannot be separated from the adult play area by an acre or so of greensward. So the problem is, clearly, how to make the available space serve for both sizes of people.

And, just as clearly, the demands of children are different from the demands of adults. Kids want different things out of a yard and, since they probably use it for more hours of the week than the adults, they're entitled to some consideration. In this brief chapter, we've tried to give you three ideas on how to make your yard suitable for both you and your children.

Around and Around in a Circle Garden

Children seem to love to go around and around, whether it's on a merry-go-round or in their own backyards. Perhaps it has something to do with a feeling of speed, or the excitement of the race and the chase, or just returning again and again to the familiar. One thing is certain: A circular route in the garden can provide more amusement hours for small children than any number of swings or slides.

This fact can influence the design of a garden, particularly a small one with more demands on each square foot of space than it can possibly satisfy. It has to be attractive all year, useful for entertaining, easily maintained and adaptable to the children so they will be content to play at home a good part of the time.

The circular grass area pictured here is simple but highly satisfactory to the whole family. It is defined by a concrete border, which serves as a mowing band for easier care and a circular route for trikes, wagons and skates.

In the larger photo, a large garden contains a circular form which is used to accent an oak tree and separate the activities of the sand box from the play equipment. The concrete path keeps the sand and tanbark from mixing too freely and is wide enough to allow for free-wheeling when the children's tricycle races are on.

To provide a ring-around race track for playing children. What could be more convenient?

Designed for Mr. & Mrs. William Barrieau, Fresno, Calif.

To encircle and accent the oak tree.

Designed for Mr. & Mrs. Howard Hickingbotham, Hillsborough, Calif.

193

When the Garden's Not for Grownups

If you are involved in the current population explosion, your garden will reflect the times. Paths will be laid out with an eye to how fast a tricycle can go around them without having to bank the turns. Flower beds, which should have delphinium and tulips, will be planted to the hardiest ground covers. Raised beds will have sand instead of camellias and trees will be planted because they are made for climbing.

When the problem becomes critical and the children more numerous, whole areas will be devoted to tanbark, concrete and sand, the balance left in grass as near the size of a football field as possible.

Later comes the pool, the teenage lanai, the arbor that can double as a setting for a garden wedding and that small addition to the quiet side of the house for you to get away from it all.

All this must be done on a rapidly decreasing lot size and in the face of rapidly increasing costs. The time does come, however, when these areas can be turned into the quiet terraces, flower borders and rose gardens that you dream of having. That is, unless you need to save them for the grandchildren.

*These yards are designed
for the present and can
become tranquil gardens
in the future.*

Designed for Mr. & Mrs. Jack Euphrat, Atherton, Calif.

195

Plan it Parallel

Most people who have built children's playgrounds on the opposite side of the house from their own patio come to realize that the very young want to be where the grown folks are. Usually they end up on their tricycles or with their buckets of sand on the adult side of the house anyway.

In this garden, the terrace and play area are side by side, separated by a seat wall which both can use. Supervision is easy. The back-and-forth screaming from child to parent and parent to child is thereby cut to a minimum.

Playgrounds are not needed forever, either. When the children grow up, go off to school or get married, this area can be made into the flower garden you never had the time for when they were young.

Today's play yard can be . . .

. . . tomorrow's garden.

Designed for Rev. & Mrs. Hugh T. Dobbins, Berkeley, Calif.

Index

Photo Credits

Maynard Parker

BACK JACKET: *Wagner garden*; TITLE PAGE: *Goldman garden*; INTRODUCTION: 2, *Part I, Gardens*; 3, *Part III, Entrances*; 4, *Part VII, Decks*; 5, *Part IX, Children's Play Areas*. GARDENS: 10-11, *Douglas Garden*; 12, *Euphrat, Sr. Garden*; 15, *Gerow Garden*; 16, *Erdman Garden*; 17, *Erdman Garden*; 21, *Menefee Garden*; 23, *Henderson Garden*; 25, *Corbus Garden*; 29, *Richards Garden*; 31; 32; 33, *Fahrney Garden*; 37, *Bradley Garden*; 41, *Packard Garden*; 43, *Berrigan Garden*; 47, *Gratton Garden*. REMODELING GARDENS: 56-7, *Sinton Garden*; 67, *Sullivan Garden*; 69, *Willard Garden*; 71, *Schroll Garden*; 73, *Metcalf Garden*. ENTRANCES: 81, *Euphrat Garden*; 82, *Robinette Garden*; 83, *Bennett Garden*; 85, *Richer Garden*; 87, *Ford Garden*; 88, *Hume Garden*. FENCES, SCREENS, STAIRS: 91, *Gerow Garden*; 93, *Blackwood Garden*; 93, *Irving Garden*; 100, *Lucas Garden*; 102, *Ruskin Garden*; 103, *Hills Garden*; 103, *Hoefer Garden*; 104-5, *Banons Garden*; 111, *Steps*; 112, *Fahrney Garden*. TREES: 115, *Murphy Garden*; 123, *De Hart Garden*. SWIMMING POOLS: 141, *Wagner Garden*; 146, *Lyon Garden*. DECKS: 155, 157, *Fahrney Garden*; 157, *Stern Garden*; 160, *Erving Garden*; 162-3, *Day Garden*; 165, *Day Garden*; 167, *Miller Garden*; 169, *Sears Garden*; 171, *(after)*; 171, *(after) De Hart Garden*; 173, *(after) McGuire Garden*. WORK AND STORAGE: 175; 178, *Johnson III Garden*; 179, *Johnson III Garden*; 180; 181; 182; 183. CHILDREN'S PLAY AREAS: 190, *Hickingbotham Garden*; 193, *Waters Garden*; 195, *Phelps Garden*; 196, *Dobbins Garden*.

Thomas D. Church

INTRODUCTION: 5, *Part VIII, Work and Storage*. GARDENS: 14, *Gerow Garden*; 19, *Church Garden*; 24, *Edwards Garden*; 36, *Bradley Garden*; 38, *Albert Garden*; 41, *De Guigne Garden*; 48, *Lall Garden*. REMODELING GARDENS: 51, *Van Strum Garden*; 55, *Field Garden*; 58-9, *Langdon Garden*; 60, *Wallace Garden*; 62-3, *Almaden Wineries Garden*; 66, *Sullivan Garden*; 68, *Willard Garden*; 70, *Schroll Garden*; 74-5-6, *Church Garden*. ENTRANCES: 87, *Eyre Garden*; 88, *Hume Garden*. FENCES, SCREENS, STAIRS: 91, *Gerow Garden*; 96, *Bradley Garden*; 98, *Witter Garden*; 107, *Banons Garden*; 107; 110, *Steps*. TREES: 119, *Helmholz Garden*; 120-1, *Davison Garden*; 123, *De Hart Garden*; 127, *Rheem Garden*. SWIMMING POOLS: 136, *Phillips Garden*; 151, *Davies Garden*; 168, *before*; 170, *before, Sears Garden*; 170, *before*; 173, *before*. WORK AND STORAGE: 176; 182; 185.

Bruce Harlow

INTRODUCTION: 1, *Thomas D. Church*. GARDENS: 27, *Walker Garden*; 39, *Albert Garden*; 44, *Berrigan Garden*. REMODELING GARDENS: 52-3, *Walker Garden*. SWIMMING POOLS: 149, *Bodman Garden*. DECKS: 158-9, *French Garden*; 167, *Bechtel Garden*; 174, *Blair Garden*. WORK AND STORAGE: 186-7-8.

Morley Baer

JACKET PHOTO of *Brooke Garden*. INTRODUCTION: 5, *Part V, Trees*; 6, *Part VI, Swimming Pools*. GARDENS: 35, *Wattis Garden*. REMODELING GARDENS: 61, *Wallace Garden*. ENTRANCES: 79-80, *Kelly Garden*. TREES: 117, *Packard Garden*. SWIMMING POOLS: 142, *Thieriot Garden*; 139, *Kelly Garden*; 139, *Fritts Garden*; 145, *De Guigne Garden*; 150, 152, *Kelly Garden*.

Photo Credits (continued)

John Robinson

INTRODUCTION: 4, *Part IV, Trees, Fences, Screens, Stairs.* GARDENS: 13, *Euphrat, Sr. Garden*; 27, *Turner Garden*; 30, *Plants on Steps.* FENCES, SCREENS, STAIRS: 97, *Bradley Garden*; 111, *Steps.* TREES: 124, *Hawkins Garden.*

Rondal Partridge

GARDENS: 10-11, *Wolff Garden.* FENCES, SCREENS, STAIRS: 105, *Wallace Garden*; 108, *Robinette Garden.* TREES: 125, *Earl Garden.*

Philip Fein

FENCES, SCREENS, STAIRS: 109, *Duff Garden.* WORK AND STORAGE: 177. CHILDREN'S PLAY AREAS: 192, *Carpenter Garden.*

Karl F. Riek

GARDENS: 34, *Wattis Garden.* REMODELING GARDENS: 64, *MacDonald Garden.*

Ernest Braun

FENCES, SCREENS, STAIRS: 92, *Euphrat Garden.* SWIMMING POOLS: 137, *Mein, Jr. Garden.* CHILDREN'S PLAY AREAS: 193, *Euphrat Garden.*

Emelie D. Nicholson

GARDENS: 42, *Salzenstein Garden.* FENCES, SCREENS, STAIRS: 95, *Salzenstein Garden.*

Ezra Stoller

GARDENS: 20, *Stockstrom Garden.*

Roger Sturtevant

SWIMMING POOLS: 135, *Saroni Garden.*